Overcome Negativity

How to Manage Negative Thoughts. Strategies to Prevent Anxiety and Depression. Practical Guide to Change Your Mind and Improve Your Life.

Table of Contents

Introduction

Congratulations on purchasing *Overcome Negativity* and thank you for doing so.

You're tired of fighting against the constant stream of negative thoughts that just won't seem to leave you alone.

You're tired of focusing on your imperfections.

You're tired of always being worried that something could go wrong.

You're tired of worrying that no one loves you.

You're tired. It's exhausting to feel like you always have to fight to stay happy. It is even harder to feel like you're missing out on opportunities because of the pessimistic thoughts that keep holding you back. You've probably spent so long trapped in a mental cycle of negativity that it has now become a bad habit you're struggling to break free from.

We don't think about it often, and we rarely discuss it with anyone else. But *everyone* has an inner voice in their head. This murmuring stream of thoughts run throughout our mind most of the time. Sometimes this inner voice can be encouraging, motivating you to reach your full potential. Other times, the inner voice can the reason for your downfall. When it is panic-ridden, pessimistic, and downright negative, we find ourselves feeling defeated and wishing for happier days.

When you allow those negative thoughts to come in and settle in your mind, they're taking up space where the good thoughts should be. There's not enough space in our mind to accommodate both elements, and you need to get rid of one to make way for the other. Specifically, get rid of negativity.

There are plenty of books on this subject on the market, thanks again for choosing this one! Every effort was made to ensure it is full of as much useful information as possible; please enjoy!

Chapter 1: Overcome Negativity

If you had to make a list, how many habits would you say have become second nature to you? The habits you do so often you don't even stop to think about it anymore. These habits have become as easy as breathing, but unfortunately, not all of them are going to be good for your health. Like negative thinking, for example. When others have started pointing out or chastise you for being too critical and too negative, you know you've got a real problem on your hands. Yes, negativity is a part of life and what keeps it balanced. There's always going to be both good and bad that you must face each day. But when other people start *describing* you as someone who is negative, that's not balanced anymore, and something needs to be done about it.

Negativity is dangerous, and it can severely hinder you in several aspects of your life. The truth is, you're never going to get very far in life when you carry this attitude with you. It doesn't matter if you think you've worked hard and should be reaping the rewards. It doesn't matter if you know all the right people. What matters is the mindset that you carry with you, the one that other people associate with you. It can hurt you both personally and professionally and trap you in an ugly cycle where the worse you feel, the more negative you become.

Defining Negativity

What does your mind tell you about the world around you? Does the world hold hope and promise? Or doom, gloom, and misery? Negativity is the overall attitude that you have about something. It is the way you see situations or people. It is the label that you put on what you see. It is the way you describe how you feel. It is all the above. The root of the problem lies in our minds and its tendency to lean toward the negative. Have you noticed how much more effort it takes to stay positive and try and keep your spirits up? Being an optimistic person feels like hard work because you're pushing your mind away from what it naturally wants to do. Most people walk around, expecting the worse subconsciously *until* they train themselves to think positive.

A negative person is difficult to get along with and unpleasant to have around. They're skeptical, and they tend to reject any constructive advice, which can be very frustrating for the people who try to help them. If you have tried helping someone out of a funk before, only to be rebuked by them every step of the way, it won't be long before you eventually throw your hands up and say *I've had enough!* Not a pleasant feeling for anyone involved.

Believe it or not, negativity is actually a survival mechanism. It is the way the human mind uses it to identify what might be wrong in certain situations so we can protect ourselves from danger. For example, when we see a dangerous animal in the wild. Our brain understands that this is a negative situation where we could potentially end up getting hurt, and the survival mechanism warns us not to get involved, so we don't risk getting hurt. Negativity used as a survival mechanism is alright, but allowing this mechanism to become the primary way to live is *not alright*. We were not meant to live in a constant state of negativity or use it to develop connections and relationships with others. Negativity shouldn't be allowed to grow strong enough that it starts to control and take over. When you live a life where focusing on weaknesses instead of strengths becomes your default mode, you're a pessimist who will always struggle to find happiness and fulfillment in life. Those elements cannot exist in a mind that is ruled by an attitude that sees the world as a glass half empty.

The Origin of Negative Thoughts

Our thoughts are the byproduct of the established thought patterns we have. These thought patterns are related to the belief system we hold. It could be about anything from confidence, self-esteem, productivity, career, relationships, finances, anything. You could be in danger of being more negative than you should if:

- You complain. A lot.
- You're sarcastic. A lot.
- You criticize. A lot.
- You blame others for anything bad that happens, but you never blame yourself. Not even once.
- You're drawn to drama like a moth to a flame.
- You have the victim mentality, and others have pointed it out to you too.
- Expecting the worse is your modus operandi.
- You tend to take everything personally and make an issue out of it.
- You dwell for hours, days, weeks, or months on bad news.

- You feel depressed.
- Your social circle consists of negative individuals too.

The effects of this kind of thinking can be disastrous. Negativity breeds more negativity. It's a contagious emotion, and the chronic stress associated with it can have detrimental effects on your health. Physically, emotionally, and mentally. The danger is that you don't realize it's starting to take over and the way it is affecting you until it's too late sometimes and you start experiencing the following side effects:

- Binge-eating or emotional eating
- Poor nutrition or not eating enough
- Rapid weight gain or weight loss (damaging to your vital organs)
- Personal and professional relationships start to fall apart
- Self-criticism
- Irrational fears
- Depression
- Anxiety
- High blood pressure
- Mood disorders

How to Deal with and Eliminate Negativity

The problem with negativity is you're not the only one affected by it. Everyone around you is too. It affects your family, your relationships, your colleagues, your friends, and anyone you interact with frequently. Those who cultivate a negative lifestyle are always guaranteed to experience more stress and illnesses because their bodies are affected by it. They are bound to experience fewer opportunities in life too. Even when opportunities do come knocking, they rarely get answered. Negativity produces all sorts of excuses and not enough action.

It's going to take a great deal of effort to overcome negativity. Positive and negative thoughts are two forces that exist within us all. They'll constantly be battling for your attention, and if you want to become someone who's positive, you're going to have to find the willpower you need to channel your energy towards positivity. The stronger force will be the one that wins out at the end of the day.

Getting rid of negativity is a challenge, and you need to be mentally prepared for that right from the start. Beginning this process with the assumption that is going to be easy enough or that results are going to happen overnight is only setting yourself up for disappointment. Patience is a necessity that you carry out the following steps to eliminate negativity from your life:

- **Creating Some Distance** - Start creating distance between anything negative that exists in your life right now. Like breaking up from a bad relationship, you must begin separating yourself bit by bit by trimming out any element in your life that is not doing you any favors. Stay away from negative people and influences so they don't have a chance to fester in your mind. There's no exception to this rule, not even people. Toxic individuals are now the people you need to stay away from. If they happen to be family members you can't exactly cut ties with, choose to spend as little time as possible in their presence. Anyone who is contributing to your negativity is someone you must distance yourself from.

- **Watch Your Feelings** - During the moments where you've got no choice but to be around toxic family members, watch your feelings when you're around them. As soon as you notice that your mood is swinging towards the negative side, excuse yourself and walk away before your emotion starts to get out of control. You don't have to feel bad about it either. Chances are you're not the only one in your family who feels this way.

- **Don't Feel Guilty** - This is your life and you owe it to yourself to put your happiness first. You don't need to feel bad or guilty about choosing to remove the toxic people from your life. No one should have the power to stop you from being happy. Doing what is best for you can be *the best thing* you end up doing. Leave the guilt at the door; there's nothing wrong with wanting to put your best interest first.

- **Avoid Arguing** - You'll never win an argument with negative people. The only guaranteed outcome is you're going to end up even more miserable than when you started. Another reason why you need to work on eliminating the toxic people from your life is that you'll get drawn into their unnecessary drama. Minimize the time you spend with them and if they try to draw you into their arguments, walk away.

- **Positive Replacement** - Positive thoughts and negative thoughts are like yin and yang. For every negative thought that your mind can churn out, there's a positive counter to it. All you need to do now is replace those negative thoughts with positive ones.

- **Thought Pattern Recognition** - There's a pattern that indicates when you're starting to fall into a negative pattern of thought. The indicator is when your beliefs start to become black and white with no grey area or middle ground. Other indicators include when you start catastrophizing, overgeneralizing or making predictions about the future, none of which are optimistic.

- **Put A Stop to Complaining** - It's not going to get you anywhere. Complaining doesn't change the situation, it doesn't fix it and it doesn't offer any long-term solution. The more you complain, the worse you feel. It's not productive and this is one toxic element you need to commit to stopping.

- **Avoid Gossiping** - Another bad habit that breeds negativity is gossip. It's toxic behavior, and the things that are said could cause some serious damage. Toxic individuals thrive on this activity because misery loves company.

- **Stop Assumptions** - Trying to assume or read someone else's mind is only feeding into the fears and anxieties that exist in your mind. When you assume without looking at the facts, you're feeding into your sense of panic. When you panic, emotions get out of control and this rarely means you're focusing on the positive. Never assume, but instead try to look at the facts in front of you.

Using Your Brain to Save You

Most people will complain at least once a minute in an average conversation. At least, according to research. Complaining is addictive, especially since our brain already tends to lean toward the negative already.

Complaining feels a lot more enjoyable than exerting extra effort trying to remain positive. Naturally, we want to do what feels easier and less like an uphill battle. The human mind is one that prefers efficiency and easy. If it can, it will always choose what feels natural and easier.

Since the brain does not like to work any harder than it has to, it like repetition. Repeated behavior allows the neurons of the brain to branch out and ease the information flow. When you complain repeatedly, it makes it easier for the brain to keep doing the same thing next time. Repetitive complaining soon becomes habitual and it rewires your brain so complaining becomes even easier as you continuously indulge in this habit. In doing so, you're strengthening your brain's negative bias, making it easier to see everything that is wrong with the world around you, regardless of how many good things may be happening too.

Your brain needs to be saved from this destruction. Stanford University's research indicates that when you complain, you're shrinking your brain's hippocampus. This is a critical area of the brain since it is responsible for intelligent thought and problem-solving. Our subconscious mind is a powerful tool, and we're the ones responsible for teaching it everything it knows. We're constantly feeding our subconscious with information. *What* is gets fed with is entirely up to you. Choose to feed it negativity and you'll become a negative person and vice versa. Because so much of the subconscious thought happens on autopilot, we're not thinking about it as much as we should be. We don't pay attention to how detrimental and damaging these thoughts can be until we wake up one morning and wonder who we became so negative. Believing that your negative thoughts are true without *challenging* them is how you gradually develop a negative mindset that can be hard to shift.

In the 20th-century, Napoleon Hill first pioneered the idea of positive thinking when he observed that the subconscious mind does not distinguish between destructive and constructive thoughts. Hill believed that the mind is capable of translating a thought driven by fear into reality as much as it can translate a thought driven by faith or courage into a positive outcome. Therefore, it is up to us to make the distinction. How do we discern between the thoughts? By asking which thought best serves our wellbeing. The ones that don't?

Well, those are the negative ones that are better left discarded. Hill summed it up nicely with his perspective.

Essentially, the subconscious mind is like a storage room. These are where all your past experiences and memories reside, both good and bad. Only when you dive deeper into your subconscious do you then realize what your core beliefs are. This also happens to be where you begin weeding out the positive thoughts from the negative ones. Until you do, you will constantly be at risk of getting trapped in negative thinking patterns. When a negative thought pops into your mind, you must *question* that thought. It's the only way to discover why you feel a certain way. Dive deeper into your subconscious to find the underlying belief that leads to the way you're feeling. To overcome negative thinking, you can't merely skim the surface of your thoughts and hope that'll be enough. You need to dig deep so you can tackle the problem at its core.

As for the conscious mind, this part of the brain monitors the thoughts that come up. It filters these thoughts, and it is the conscious mind that decides which thoughts get rejected and which ones make the cut. The thoughts that your conscious mind chooses to accept or reject will be based on *which thoughts appear to be useful.* Useful in terms of their sense of self, or useful in terms of identity. When you indulge in a negative thought about yourself, you're opening the door wide open and telling that thought *"come on in and stay here."* When you accept that thought as your reality, it gets stored in your subconscious mind. When a relatable situation comes along, you tap into that thought and it feeds into the preconceived notion you developed earlier. For example, when you believe that you are fat. That thought gets stored away, and each time a situation comes up that causes you to be body-conscious, it will evoke negative feelings since you already don't feel good about yourself. Each time you connect with these negative thoughts, you're feeding into all the unhealthy emotions you feel. Your belief becomes "fixed" that you are fat, and you continue to hold that belief *until you start to question or challenge it.*

How to Feel Happy and Present

It's easy to feel grateful every day if we only pause long enough to focus on the good things in life. No matter how miserable life may appear to be, it's not as bad as it seems. There's a silver lining if you look hard enough. Remember the yin and yang balance? There's always a positive counterpart, only most of the time we're too caught up in the negativity to see it. The unrealistic expectations we put in place certainly don't help matters either. We want the world to be the way we *think* it should be. Anything that does not go your way gets labeled as bad. We might not want to admit it, but deep down most of us have a sense of entitlement. We feel that the universe should revolve according to the expectations we have set. We think about our needs and wants, and what those don't get fulfilled *exactly* the way you want them too, your unhappiness sets you up for a life of misery and negativity. We fail to appreciate the little nuances of life. When things don't seem to go your way, you begin thinking that you're not as "lucky" or "fortunate" as others and negativity start to fester.

Being grateful each day is one of the many ways to train yourself to feel happy and present at the moment, regardless of what your situation might be. Adopt this approach and you'll open yourself up to the idea of positivity. You begin to feel grateful. For every little thing in your life, from being able to grab your favorite cup for coffee for the day to the smooth traffic you experienced on the way to work. Instead of finding a list of things to complain about, you've got a list of things to be grateful for. Since the latter puts a smile on your face, it's safe to say that it is the better list to have.

Feeling happy and present despite the negativity that surrounds your life can be done if you work through the following steps one at a time:

- **Keep A Journal of Everything You're Grateful For** - It's easier than trying to make a list off the top of your head. Every morning let your new ritual be to write down at least three things that you're grateful for right from the start. This encourages you to start your day off on a positive note right from the very beginning. The things you're grateful for don't have to be fancy or outrageous. They just have to be things that put a smile on your face. Things that remind you and make you say, *"You know what? I am very blessed after all."* This way, you're training your brain every morning to focus on positivity, and once this becomes a habit, it will be effortless.

- **Don't Be Afraid to Laugh at Yourself** - It doesn't have to be a bad thing. People make mistakes, and sometimes those mistakes are funny. If we didn't make mistakes, we're no better than robots. Take life a little less seriously and things won't look so bleak all the time. Sometimes you do make funny mistakes and it's okay to laugh about it. If it lightens the mood, why not? It's better to be laughing than sitting in a corner feeling miserable and sorry for yourself. Learn not to take everything personally; it's not always about you.

- **Rewiring Your Mind** - How? With positive affirmations. Negativity is a great advocate of the phrase *I can't*. To rewire your brain, you're going to have to remove the last letter from that word. Positive affirmations that remind you of what you're capable of can be empowering. *I can do this. I can manage that deadline. I can handle that business meeting. I can find the silver lining. I can find the lesson in this experience. I CAN*. That's the keyword your affirmations need to be based on to remind you that you are the one who is always in control, no matter what havoc your emotions are playing on you.

- **Say I Love You -** When was the last time you told someone you loved how you felt about them? Family, partners, spouses, boyfriends, girlfriend, children, friends, anyone. When was the last time you told them you loved and appreciated them? Telling someone how you feel reminds you that there is love in your life. Everything else that is going on is easily manageable when you've got love and support on your side.

- **Saying Thank You -** Part of being a more grateful person is to say thank you for every little thing. Whenever someone does something nice for you, say thank you. No matter how small it is, it's nice to hear appreciation. We're so busy these days many of us don't stop long enough to say thank you anymore. But a simple, two-letter word can go a long way in making someone's day feel better.

Chapter 2: Prevent Anxiety

Despite the way that it makes you feel, anxiety is not your enemy. It is your body's natural response when it is undergoing stress. Anxiety is normal, and it only becomes a problem when the brain is not processing this whirlwind of emotions in a healthy way.

Anxiety can feel like it's happening all at once, but there are signs leading up to the moment when your anxiety becomes full on. For example, the first indicator is when you start to obsess about a single thought. Or maybe several thoughts for that matter. You repeat these thoughts on an endless loop, and this is a sure sign of anxiety when you find it difficult to let go of that thought and move on. You know it's making you feel distressed, yet you can't stop thinking about it. This leads to the second indicator, where you try to control the situation and over-plan. When you find that you can't control everything, you start to panic and become decidedly more emotional and anxious over the elements that are out of your hands.

Your anxious thoughts seem to take control of your life to the point it's stopping you from getting a good night's sleep. That's when you know you've hit the third indicator that alerts you to the presence of anxiety. Tossing and turning in bed worrying is not a sign of healthy behavior. Your anxious thoughts are like a dog that is fascinated with chasing and catching its tail. You'll keep going round and round in circles without ever finding a proper solution. It's exhausting and pointless. Other indicators that signal you might be dealing with more anxiety than you realized include:

- **A Routine That Is Slowly Getting More Rigid** - Having a routine can be a good thing. It keeps you organized and productive, and you get a lot more done in a day when you've got a routine to follow. Anxiety can be difficult to spot in this case and it creeps into your routine so subtly you don't even notice its presence at first. When you start noticing that it's getting harder to try new things or break out of your routine, you could be on the verge of an anxiety attack and it's starting to become a hindrance. The emotional part of the brain is called the *limbic system,* and this part of the brain floods the more rational part of the brain known as the *neocortex*. When this block happens, it's stopping you from brainstorming alternative solutions when you're feeling overwhelmed with stress, thus explaining why it is difficult to think rationally when you're under pressure.

- **Every Little Thing Is Setting You Off** - The smallest things are starting to aggravate you or set you off. What never used to bother you before now seems like a big deal and something to stress over. You blame your irritation and anger on a person or situation, not realizing that perhaps anxiety is the one making you feel this way. Since *both* anxiety and anger are responsible for triggering the *fight or flight* response mechanism, it is easy to mistake both these emotions. Without identifying the triggers, you won't be able to tell which problem is the one that needs fixing. If it's anger, you need to address what's making you angry and its anxiety, acknowledge that perhaps these emotions are there to protect you. You don't have to act on your anxiety or let it get out of control. With proper emotional regulation, anxiety doesn't have to be the enemy.

- **Your Appetite Has Changed -** One of the physical ways anxiety affects your body is through your appetite. When you're stressed out, worried or feeling anxious, thinking about your regular mealtimes is going to be the last thing on your mind. When cortisol (stress hormone) is flooding your system, your appetite is going to be the one that takes flight first. You've probably noticed you're not eating the way you should but brushed it off and thought it was probably because you're "too busy" or "had a lot of things on your mind." Little did you realize anxiety could be the underlying culprit in this scenario, and not eating properly is only going to aggravate the situation and make you feel worse.

Believe You Have the Power to Be Happy

It's hard to imagine being happy when anxiety is the one in control. Maybe you've been dealing with it for so long it feels like you've got no control over your life anymore and everything feels like it's out of your hands.

You don't know what to expect, and when things happen, you don't know how to react. Having no control over your emotions, you try to control everything else around you, including other people and situations in an attempt to gain some sense of control again. When you realize that's not working, it fills you with even more anxiety and the cycle keeps going.

A lot of the anxious feelings we have stems from the fear of the unknown. Life is not predictable. You can plan and prepare as best you can, but life has a plan of its own. You can never be too sure what's going to happen next and feeling powerless makes anxiety feel like an impossible emotion to cope with. You feel disconnected with yourself and wake up each morning wondering what's the point of all this? The more you try to control your behavior or actions, the worse you seem to feel. You feel like screaming out loud whenever someone tells you to "get over it" or "it's not a big deal." They have *no idea* what's going on in your mind. It feels like your life is taking you on a roller-coaster ride, except that you have no idea where you're going to end up and it's causing you a great deal of stress in the process.

With all this going on, how do we find the willpower to be happy? How do we find the *belief* that we *deserve* to be happy, too? Humans feel happy when they have some level of control in their lives. In fact, they *need* this control and the research relating to humans and the need for control has been around for a long time. In 1959, Robert White in his research suggested that all of us have a fundamental need to establish or exert some extent of control on the world around us. People *need* to believe that they are capable of producing the results that they want, or there would be very little motivation to face the challenges they come up against. If no one believed that they had the power and control to make a difference, no one would get anything done. Therefore, the perception of control we have has likely evolved and adapted for survival. The need for control is primal, and it exists for the sake of our mental health and wellbeing. The research done on the framework of perceived control confirmed that it was a major contributor to our physical and mental health and a strong predictor of the kind of achievements we go on to accomplish.

It is safe to say that a sense of control is a normal, maybe even a necessary part of the overall human experience. Living with the belief that external forces have more control over our lives than we do ends up creating a lot of anxiety. But to feel happier, we need to focus *less* on trying to control our external environment and *more* on the power of choice. That presents an interesting dilemma. To give up trying to control everything in our external surroundings (going against the primal need for control) is something many people struggle with. Especially those who deal with anxiety. We need to give up control, *yet* we need this control to be happy. Feeling like fate is not within your hands makes the situation feel a lot worse, but the truth is, life will *never be fully* in your control. What do we do then?

That's where the power of choice comes in. You have a lot of choices to think about when the unexpected happens. You *choose* what you want to do next. You *choose* the way you want to respond to it. You *choose* how much power the effects of that even have on your emotional and mental wellbeing. You *choose* whether to let it go or hold on to what has happened and think about it repetitively. You *choose* whether to learn from the experience or let it negatively impact you. In that sense, you're in charge of choosing your happiness. You don't have to throw your hands up and say, "I give up!"

that choice resides with you too. Everything comes down to choice, including your happiness.

If you choose *not* to let the situation make you feel miserable, it won't. If you choose *not* to see an outcome as a failure, you won't. Once you learn how to redirect that need for trying to control your external environment inward and focus on the power of choice instead, everything will change. You're still indulging that primal need for control but in a different and more productive way this time. Instead of driving yourself crazy trying to micromanage your entire life, focus on what you can choose to do to feel better instead. When channeled productively, choices can be a strong correlation to the positive outcomes you experience. Instead of allowing yourself to feel miserable or that life is completely hopeless, remind yourself that there *are* some things that are still within your control and it all boils down to the choices you make:

- Choose to be happy
- Choose to take better care of yourself
- Choose not to let a bad situation negatively impact you because there is always a silver lining and lesson to be learned in every experience

- Choose the way you're going to respond.

Focusing on controlling the *right* areas is how you make a difference and the way you redirect that need for control in a healthier, more productive manner. You might not have control over *everything* in life, but you do have control over your perception and your decision to be happy.

Take Control of Your Life

Regardless of how frequently it happens or how overbearing it seems to be, the power to take control of your life again is never out of your hands. Anxiety only makes it *feel* like you don't have any control, but you do. You *do* have all the power you need, no matter what anxiety tries to convince you of. Because anxiety is a part of who we are, it will always come knocking at your door now and then. Even when you have learned to control it. When it does, stay in control with the following techniques:

- **What's Your Source?** - What is the source of your anxiety? This question doesn't get asked often enough. The focus is on how emotional and overwhelmed you feel because that seems bigger than everything else. But what if you stopped to ask *what's my source?* Identify the source and you'll be able to think of a more long-term and effective solution to solving the problem once and for all. If you don't know what your sources are, try keeping a thought journal. Carry it with you and track how anxious you feel over the course of the day so you can spot a pattern. There are other ways of tracking your mood throughout the day too if you don't feel like carrying a journal around with you. Make a note on your phone with one of the many available apps. At the end of the day, reflect on the day you had and look back at how often you felt anxious. When did the episodes occur and what triggered it? You might be surprised to learn what the triggers are; sometimes they could be what you least expect. There's always a cause, and when you think you've identified it, you can then work on resolving it.

- **Hit the Delete Button** - Metaphorically speaking. You need to hit the delete button in your mind on every negative thought that pops in. The second you start to change your thoughts, that change in perspective changes your life. Most of the time, we tend to invite anxiety in with the things we do. Each time you fixate on a negative thought, am embarrassing past experience, obsess about what you can't change, you're leaving the door wide open for anxiety to come waltzing in. Putting a stop is only possible when you *choose* to eliminate the bad from your mind. Hit the delete button.

- **Make Yourself Bigger Than Your Worries** - Tricking your mind into believing that you're bigger than your anxiety can make you feel a lot more confident. It's like what you would do if you noticed a physical threat. Let's say you were out hiking, and you happen to spot a wild animal who looks like it might attack you if it came any closer. You would stand taller, make yourself appear bigger, stomp your feet and make loud noises until the animal wandered off in the other direction. You don't need to do exactly that to get rid of anxiety, luckily. The approach is a lot more subtle in this context. To "make yourself seem bigger" than your worries in the case of anxiety is going to boil down to mental prowess. The first step involves smiling. Even when you don't feel like it, smile. Do it until you're no longer faking it. Your brain and your body are linked intrinsically. The change you evoke with one is going to affect the other. When you smile, you're resetting your brain's circuit breaker. Smile because there is no worry out there strong enough to bring you down. Smile because you are bigger than your worries; you simply need to remember that during the moments you need it most.

- **Put the Flames Out** - You're the firefighter and your anxious thoughts are the fire. You can put out the flames and your fire extinguisher, in this case, is deep, controlled and measured breaths. Each time you feel your thoughts starting to get the best of you, take a deep breath in, pause, release, and repeat. Breathe in harder than you normally would; it forces you to focus on what you're doing instead of focusing on what makes you anxious.

- **Put It in Perspective** - Are the things you're worried about realistic? Are they based on facts or assumptions? If it is the latter, then it's time to take back control by getting some perspective on your triggers. Most of the anxiety we feel stems from needless worry if you think about it. Can you count the number of times your projected worst-case scenario actually turned out to be true? Hardly ever or never, most like it. Then, ask yourself if these anxious thoughts are worth getting this worked up over? Is it worth losing sleep at night? Is it worth being this miserable obsessing over what you might not be able to control? If the answer is no, then put it in perspective and think about what your priorities are instead.

- **Don't Ignore the Signs** - Anxiety is your body's way of telling you something is not right, and you need to listen. It may be a response to the stress you're feeling, but if the anxiety persists long after the trigger has passed, then something needs to be done. Listen to what your body and your mind are trying to tell you before the situation escalates and gets worse. Suppressing anxiety has the same effects as a pressure cooker. It'll still be simmering beneath the surface until it reaches a point where it can no longer take it. Suppression only works short-term and when you reach the breaking point, everything is going to spill forth all at once, making things even worse.

- **Ride It Out** - Instead of trying to fight your anxiety, let it happen. Let it come and ride it out. Life is full of ups and downs, and the bad moments rarely ever last long. Trying to push against it, reject or deny your anxiety only makes it feel worse than what it is. Taking control of your life means taking things in stride as they come and remember that everything will pass in time. Even these moments of anxiety you feel.

Good Habits to Control Anxiety

Anxiety is normal. What is *not* normal about it is accepting that anxiety is something you have to "live with" and nothing can be done about it. That you're doomed to struggle through this misery alone in isolation. That is simply not true. Ignoring your problems won't make it go away and neither will it help to agonize over them. Masking the issues with medication is only a short-term solution. You need something *a lot more powerful* and stronger than that. The only *effective* way to get rid of these problems is to be proactive about it. What does proactiveness look like in this scenario? Good habits.

Good habits help you regain your confidence by addressing all the underlying discomfort that anxiety causes you. You're not alone in your struggles to overcome anxiety. There are millions of people out there going through the same thing you are. The decision to reclaim power over your life includes the cultivation of these good habits that help you manage your anxiety:

- **Be Kind to Yourself** - You need to if you're going to feel happy again. Accept the way that you feel because your emotions are part of who you are. It's not wrong to feel the way you do, and you shouldn't beat yourself up over it. Judging yourself too harshly is a bad habit that must be broken for the sake of your mental and emotional wellbeing as well as happiness. Good or bad, emotions are part of who you are. Own them. Every single one, even the ones that make you anxious. Adopt the habit of being kind to yourself because if you don't do it, who will?

- **Educating Yourself** - Not knowing exactly what you're dealing with can make a bad situation seem worse. Remember the fear of the unknown? Well, it applies within the anxiety context too. Educating yourself on your anxiety is the only way to overcome it. Make it a habit to assess each trigger and educate yourself on why you feel the way you do. Why does this trigger affect you so badly? The more information you have to go on, the easier it will become to see "Oh, that's not too bad after all." Maybe your triggers are not as bad as they initially seemed, now that you're armed with knowledge.

- **Pay It Forward** - One way to counter the negative emotions is to do something good that lifts your spirits. Empower yourself by doing something good for someone else without expecting anything in return. If you can do something good for someone, why not? If it makes their day better and puts a smile on their face. Focusing on doing good takes your mind away from the worries for a moment.

- **Live Healthier** - Making health a priority is an underrated habit. But this one simple change can do more for your overall health and wellbeing than any form of medication ever will. Medication masks the symptoms, and masking your anxiety is not going to make it go away. Everything you feel will still be there and becoming dependent on medication is not the best solution to take either. Take your meds when you need to but learn not to rely on them. Adopt a healthier lifestyle so you can wean yourself off the medication. Natural self-help techniques are always a better approach to take.

- **Healing Your Energy** - It may sound like a lot of mumbo jumbos, but don't discredit it until you've tried it. Those dealing with anxiety that is caused by trauma stands to benefit from this approach the most. Healing your energy is a part of the recovery process since anxiety stems from within. Our body is made up of energy centers known as *chakras*, and anxiety throws these energy forces off balance. If your anxiety is caused by trauma, don't be afraid of confronting that pain. Look at the past moments and what triggered the anxiety you felt. This may be a painful exercise for many, but it is a necessity, nonetheless. Combined with educating yourself about the anxiety, it can lead to moments of revelation that allow deeper healing to take place.

Chapter 3: Prevent Depression

Feeling down or miserable occasionally is not uncommon. It's the way we respond and cope with the events or situations that take place in our lives. Our emotions need an outlet. There may be times every now and then when you're feeling blue or sad for no reason. It happens and generally, it is nothing to worry about since the feelings pass with time. Clinical depression, however, is another matter entirely and there is a very *big* difference between feeling sad every now and then and being depressed.

Depression is intense and usually lasts a lot longer than a couple of days. When you become so miserable it's starting to impact your ability to function in your daily routine; it is important that you take this seriously. The problem is that it's not always easy to tell when someone is going through depression. The changes in their mood and behavior could happen so gradually that it is barely noticeable and therefore, the signs are easy to miss. Even harder if the person going through the emotion does not want to talk about the way they feel.

Depression is characterized by the following signs and symptoms:

- Feeling anxious and irritable
- Feeling hopeless, teary and sad
- Feeling bad about yourself and life
- Feeling isolated and alone
- Feeling tired or exhausted all the time, no matter how much rest you get
- Feeling angry or guilty
- Having thoughts where you blame yourself
- Negative self-talk and being overly critical about yourself
- Lack of motivation to do anything anymore
- Insomnia or poor-quality sleep at night
- No longer enjoying the little things that used to make you happy
- Loss of appetite or increase in appetite
- Weight loss or weight gain
- Difficulty focusing and paying attention
- Leaving the house feels like a struggle
- Substance abuse (drugs or alcohol) to "numb" the pain

Should any of the emotional or physical signs persist for longer than two weeks, you should consider seeking the advice of a professional to determine what you're dealing with. Depression comes in several forms, some of which may require treatment or medication before it gets resolved. Depression, no matter how dark the emotion may seem, is something you *can* recover from with understanding and the right kind of help.

Your Emotional Triad

Motivational speaker Tony Robbins and other psychological experts believe that three specific factors determine the way that we feel moment-to-moment. They call these three factors the *Emotional Triad,* and the three factors it is made up of are:

- Focus
- Language
- Physiology

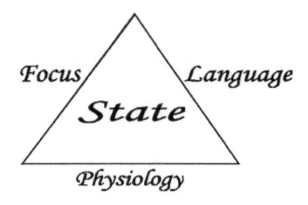

Image Source: Project Life Mastery

Focus

The first factor that decides the way you feel is what you *choose* to focus on. The mind is where it all begins. Happy, confident individuals focus on positive things in their life that make them feel this way. They ask questions that phrased in a positive way, such as *"What am I happy/thankful for today?"* They choose to think about the happy moments in their lives and fill their minds with only pleasant memories. It is what you *choose* to focus your attention on that will ultimately decide the way that you feel.

Language

The language and the words you use have the power to affect the way you feel. Hence the constant emphasis on the need for positive self-talk. Repeated negative reinforcement only serves to encourage the feelings of depression that may be starting to form. Negative talk simply does not put you in the empowering state of mind you need to be in to weather any challenge that comes your way. Pay attention to the vocabulary you use, because these statements and phrases can do a lot to control your state of mind.

Physiology

Your body feels every emotion that it goes through. The body is the first place to feel it. People who are passionate, for example, tend to speak faster and move more rapidly when they're talking about the subject they're passionate about. People who are confident speak clearly, stand taller, smile and make eye contact. People who are depressed look downward, avoid eye contact, frown, slump over and hunch their shoulders. The way that our body communicates has the ability to change the way we feel biochemically.

How People Handle the Negative Emotions They Feel

Most people have specific ways of processing and dealing with the negative emotions they feel. Some choose to avoid them; others choose to deny them. Some people choose to compete against others by making it seem like they have it worse off than anyone else. It's not uncommon to hear them say phrases like *"You think you've had a bad day? You don't even know half of what I've been through."*

The final way of dealing with negative emotions is the most effective one. People who choose to *learn* from their emotions and find better-coping strategies are the ones who become the most successful at overcoming the unhappiness they feel. That's because when they choose to learn from their emotions, they are simultaneously choosing to *change* the way they feel. This group of individuals has come to realize how the above emotional triad affects them and that they have the power to change the way they feel if they wanted to. All they have to do is act on it.

No matter which way you have been choosing to deal with your negative emotions up to this point, remember that there is always room for change. The moment you decide to change is the moment change happens. You start to bring about a shift in your emotions when you decide you want to turn things around and prevent depression from happening. That shift in your emotions, however, requires emotional intelligence.

Shifting Your Emotions

Emotional intelligence continues to be an increasingly critical and popular skill to possess. Particularly in the professional world, but it can benefit you in everyday life too. Even more so when it comes to preventing and overcoming depression and negativity. Emotional intelligence is far from a trend. Research conducted by several major companies has already compiled proof statistics wise about how emotionally intelligent employees affect the bottom line. It is a skill that increases productivity, motivation, and ultimately, a company's bottom line. Right now, it is going to be the very skill you need to bring about the necessary shift in your emotions toward the positive.

The five core pillars of emotional intelligence are *self-awareness, self-regulation, empathy, motivation, and social skills*. Each of these pillars is going to be essential in changing your perception and the way you view and handle things that happen in your life. In terms of shifting your emotions away from the negative, emotional intelligence is going to benefit you on that front because:

- **It Encourages Assertiveness** - Anxiety and depression cause many to be afraid of their emotions. As such, they have difficulty expressing and asserting the way they feel. When everything is kept bottled up inside, it makes them feel worse about themselves. Emotional intelligence encourages awareness about the way you feel, and to regulate your emotions enough so they don't have to feel more powerful than you are. You are stronger than any emotion that you feel.

- **It Encourages You to Respond, Not React** - Responding and reacting to the situations you're going through are a very different thing.

Responding negatively results in subsequent negative reactions, leading to anxiety, negativity, chronic worry and of course, depression. Emotional intelligence is the necessary skill needed to stay calm in any stressful situation. By being aware of your emotions and regulating them the way that is needed, you're able to mitigate your reactions by refraining from impulsive decisions.

- **It Encourages Self-Awareness** - This skill is the *most* important emotional intelligence skill set out of the five. To be so aware of your emotions and the way that it affects you as well as the people around you is a skill that not a lot of people have mastered. Why? Because it's not as easy as it sounds. You can't shift your emotions if you don't understand *what* it is that you're feeling. There won't be any incentive either to change the way you feel if you don't understand the way your emotions can impact the people around you. Only emotional intelligence can reveal that.

How Habits Are Formed

A lot of our thought pattern boils down to the habits we have developed. Habits are not reserved for the physical things we do alone. Habits can be the thoughts that we have trained ourselves to listen to and believe over a period of time.

From the moment we are born, we've been conditioned by our environment to behave and act in a certain way. There's a lot of trial and error that takes place as you attempt to discover what works and what doesn't. When the brain perceives something to be "too hard" to do, it will automatically resist trying to make it a habit. There's too much work involved, and our brain wants the easier route to take. Which is why staying positive is often a difficult habit to implement. It takes a lot of effort to stay positive. Our habits are formed based on the experience we go through. Physical habits are a lot easier to identify than the emotional and mental ones we carry around simply because the physical habits are easier to see. We're very visual creatures, and it is much easier to believe and be convinced about what we can see in front of us.

Identifying mental and emotional habits is the harder part of the challenge. Unhealthy mental and emotional habits like excessive worry and anxiety are not something that should be taken lightly. There have been instances where chronic worriers are so anxiety-ridden that they start to seek out harmful habits such as turning to alcohol, drugs, smoking and sometimes even overeating in a false attempt to make themselves feel better. In worst-case scenarios, their levels of anxiety and worry can be so high that it can lead to depressive and even suicidal thoughts.

Habits are formed in four stages:

- **The Cue** - Cues are the elements that trigger certain behavior. For example, when you're exposed to something you don't like to do, your anxiety gets triggered. When bad things keep happening one after another, your depression is triggered. When the deadlines keep piling on at work, your stress is triggered. When all of these happen, it cues your brain to activate its negative side and that's when the negative self-talk and unhelpful emotions that come along with it start to flood your system.

- **The Craving** - The human mind tends to be biased toward the negative. On some level, part of us could be *craving* to feel the way we do. It's strange but true. You don't want to feel miserable, yet you actively seek it out anyway. Breaking out of this habit requires you to want a *different kind* of craving. This time, you need to crave control over your emotions instead of craving scenarios or thoughts that only feed into the negativity.

- **The Response** - By this stage, you're acting out on what you were craving before. If you were craving more negativity, that's what you will be responding to. For example, when you're already stressed from trying to meet a deadline at work. Instead of taking a 5-minute break to recharge your energy levels or grabbing a cup of coffee, you choose to respond to the negative stress you're feeling by *adding* even more stress by trying to push through and keep working anyway. Before you know it, you're burned out and feeling drained already and still not satisfied with the level of work you produced.

- **The Reward** - Every habit has an end goal in mind. When you repeat the actions that lead to that same end goal, that's when it becomes a habit.

Habitual chronic worriers worry so much that they end up failing to realize worrying is doing nothing beneficial for them. Nor will they be able to control a situation or circumstance more by constantly worrying about it. When chronic worrying becomes a habit, the worrier loses all ability to see the silver lining in any situation. All they can think about and focus on are the negatives and they look at life as a glass half empty environment. Losing the ability to see the positive side of situations will increase a worrier's levels of anxiety and fear and do nothing to help quell the overwhelming sense of worry that they feel. Eventually, it becomes almost impossible to view things positively, even when there is nothing bad to think about. Worriers don't realize that this habit is harmful and can have some serious adverse effects on their health.

Good Habits to Control Your Emotions

Trying to keep your emotions out of the equation can be tough. Emotions *are who we are* and trying to separate yourself from your feelings is not always the easiest thing in the world. Negative thoughts are unhealthy for the brain. We know that bringing emotions into the mix, especially with important decisions, can spell disaster in some cases. It takes a great deal of self-control, willpower, discipline, and emotional mastery to separate yourself from the situation and see things with level-headedness and clarity. When worrying becomes a habit, that habit becomes hard to break. Continually feeding your brain with these negative and unhealthy emotions will eventually take its toll. People who worry in excess find that they have a hard time reprogramming their minds to think more positive thoughts, and this becomes increasingly harder the more worrying becomes a habit. If you are guilty of worrying excessively, it's time to reprogram your brain and force yourself to focus on the more positive things in life before it's too late.

Certain emotions, like anger, anxiety, and depression, for example, can completely stunt their ability to make sound, grounded, and rational decisions.

Emotions need to be regulated, and these are the habits to begin adopting on your way to emotional intelligence:

- **Step Back and Assess** - You can *feel* when your emotions are starting to get the best of you through self-awareness. By being mindful and paying attention to your body and feelings, you can tell when the moment happens where you begin spiraling out of control. The way you feel is triggered by something, emotions rarely ever come out of nowhere and immediately go from zero to a full-blown emotional outburst. Maybe you're already feeling anxious about something, or you were feeling depressed and miserable for weeks now but never noticed the build-up. No matter what emotion you may be feeling, there is always a trigger to it. Step back and assess what's bothering you. It sounds easy enough, but you'd be surprised at how difficult some people find this to be.

- **Forming Boundaries** - To overcome negativity, anxiety, depression and any other mental health issue you may be dealing with that is deeply impacting you, you need to create boundaries. Boundaries are not something reserved for toxic individuals alone; it should be something you enforce with yourself too. Boundaries help protect your mental and emotional fragility by teaching you to prioritize yourself. To encourage you not to allow these negative emotions to swarm in on your mind. Just like you would limit your interaction with a toxic individual, you're going to now limit your exposure to negativity. One example of an emotional boundary is putting a stop of negative self-talk. Or any kind of talk that slowly eats away at your confidence levels. Any emotion that will push your buttons or negatively impact your mood should not be allowed to cross the threshold. This is where emotional intelligence once again comes into play.

- **Respond without Reacting** - You can respond to the emotions you feel without reacting outwardly to it. Once more, emotional intelligence shows what a useful tool it can be. Before you respond to anything that you go through with immediate anxiety and negativity as your default reaction, think about the situation rationally. Is it really as bad as it seems? Are you looking at all the facts first or leading with your heart instead of your head? Would it have helped if you walked away and cleared your head for a minute before coming back to the situation? 90% of the time things feel a lot worse than they really are *because* of the way we choose to respond. The respond without reacting technique means you're assessing the situation internally and acknowledging the way you feel, but on the outside, you try to maintain and calm and cool composure without giving away how you feel. This gets easier to do with emotional intelligence, which gives you the capacity to (even in your highly emotional state) to understand the consequences of your actions.

- **Attention Training** - The mind is a mental muscle, and the only way it is going to get stronger is through exercise. The same way our bodies get stronger when we put it through rigorous exercise routines. Those routines are not easy, but eventually, you get there and the same philosophy applies in your mind too. It's easy to get stuck in a depression or anxiety spiral, as you probably already experienced firsthand. The endless rumination leaves you stuck and struggling to move forward. The way we habitually think will eventually shape the way we habitually feel. Negativity is like a force of gravity, it pulls you in and once you're in, it's hard to claw your way back out again without putting up a good fight. To resist the negativity, pull, you must strengthen your mind's mental muscle. More specifically, strengthen your ability to focus and pay attention. There's not much you can go about the thoughts that come and go through your mind, but what you *can do* is pay attention. The stronger your attention is, the better you'll be at focusing on thoughts that are beneficial to you instead. Your mood will dramatically improve because of it. Mindfulness meditation is one of the most effective forms of attention training, and all it takes is 5-minutes out of your day to do it.

- **Talking to Yourself** - As strange as this sounds, talking to an audience of one (yourself) can be surprisingly effective and a good habit to cultivate to keep your emotions in check. The act of saying things out loud reaffirms them in your mind. Saying positive statements out loud, for example, makes them seem a lot more definitive than merely repeating those phrases in your mind. When you say something out loud, you're indirectly forcing your thoughts to slow down long enough so you can repeat the phrases aloud. Why? Because we can think as quickly as we speak or write. This means your negative thoughts won't have enough time to pick up the speed they need to send your emotions into a tailspin. Slowing it down long enough to buy you the time you need to process these thoughts too. Whether you're saying it out loud to yourself and writing your thoughts down on paper, slowing down your thoughts makes you more aware. With enough time to put some distance between you and your thoughts, you get a fresh perspective on your emotional triggers. This perspective could turn out to be exactly what you need to disengage from your negative thoughts and do what you need to change them.

- **Thought Reframing** - Reframing your thoughts can significantly help to minimize and reduce your worries over time because you're getting into the habit of changing your perspective on the situations you're presented with, viewing them in a more positive light which lets you know you are capable of handling it and there's no reason to worry so much about it. Reframing helps to remind you of all the positive attributes and skills that you have, the tools that you need to handle the challenging moments that show up in your life. Our worries stem from assuming the worst of every situation, and reframing helps to turn that around and helps you realize that things are not as bad as they initially seem. With less worry comes fewer reasons to be depressed and unhappy. The reframing process will do wonders for your life if you start practicing it daily and make it a habit. It's going to take some effort at first, of course, just like Eventually, you will see what a big difference just reframing your thoughts and changing the way you think about things can do for you.

Chapter 4: Manage Negative Thoughts

How do we free ourselves from negative thoughts? That's probably a question we've thought about several times over. It's the same question anyone out there who is dealing with negativity and struggling to overcome it will have. The presupposition we have is that we're "trapped" by the unhelpful thoughts we have. Look at the phrasing of that sentence. The word "trapped" alone is enough to make you feel like you're in an inescapable prison of your mind. To free yourself from this proverbial prison, you need to understand what's going on. *Really* understand.

How do we learn to pay more attention to success and less to the setbacks? How do we spend less emotional bandwidth on the negative thoughts and more on the thoughts that are going to empower and uplift us? Those are really good questions to think about. These are questions everyone can relate to. No matter who you are, how experienced you may be, how successful or how accomplished you are, staying positive *is a struggle*. It's not easy, and anyone who tells you that it is easy is either kidding themselves or trying to kid you. You could do 100 good or positive things in a day, and all it takes is that *one* negative comment, *one* person who rejects you, *one* thing going wrong to erase the other 100 good deeds that went on today.

We need 100 reasons to be happy but only one reason is all we need to feel miserable. Unfortunately, this is how the brain is wired. We're programmed to take in the bad and ignore the good. This ancient way of how the brain wires date back to our earliest ancestors. Back then, being wired this way helped us stay alive for the next several centuries. Since then, Mother Nature continues to train our minds to overestimate threats while simultaneously underestimating opportunities. Not such a helpful trait in this day and age since we no longer need to rely on it to escape predators that might eat us. Back in the day, the hair-trigger reaction to immediately think negative and flee kept us alive. Today, this same reaction keeps us feeling miserable and awful because the lives we lead today are so different.

The mind is *not designed* to do things that feel uncomfortable, scary or difficult. Our brains are designed to *protect us* from those things and in order to change and to do all the things you know you want to accomplish, you're going to *have to do things that are difficult, challenging, uncomfortable and scary.* Nothing good in life ever comes easy. This presents a problem for all of us. How do we do things that our brain is afraid of *without* succumbing to the negative thought patterns that are bound to follow because we're doing something outside our comfort zone?

To make matters worse, negative experiences move a lot quicker into our long-term memory than positive ones do. No need to point out that negativity is terrible for your health either. If you've been living with negativity for a long time now, you've probably already felt its effects. It increases your anxiety, weakens your immune system and kills your motivation and ambition. Too often, we allow these negative thoughts to stop us in our tracks and make us doubt our abilities. Instead of using mistakes as a motivator to help propel us forward in life, we choose to let it become barriers that prevent us from doing what we need to do to improve.

There's a habit we are all guilty of. All of us with no exception, are guilty of hesitating. Sometimes you know what you want to do, or you've got an idea of what you would like to do, but you stop, and you hesitate from doing anything about it. What we don't realize is how that micro-moment of hesitation sends a stress signal to your brain. It wakes the brain up and immediately begins to think of all the things that could go wrong and give you all the excuses you need to *avoid* doing something. As soon as one negative thought starts, the rest will follow one after another and before you know it, you're feeling stuck and unable to move. Is there something that can be done to overcome this? Yes, there is. *Two* things in fact, which is to first create a shift in your thoughts and then to follow that with the cultivation of good habits that keep your mind diverted away from what it wants to do: *dwell on the negative.*

How to Bring About A Shift in Your Thoughts

All thoughts are *habitual.* If you think about it, over 90% of your daily thoughts more or less revolve around the *same thing.* They're probably the same thoughts you had yesterday, the day prior to that, and maybe even the week before. That's because our mind works by automatic conditioning. Habits are comfortable. Familiar. Therefore, they are easier to accept and repeat. If that conditioning is predominantly negative, then it makes sense that we feel "trapped" by these patterns of negative thinking that we continue to engage in. We don't pay attention to the fact that we're feeding our minds with thoughts all the time. These internal messages can either reprimand or inspire. Which one they do depends on what we allow to happen.

Bad things happen, that's a part of life and the way it works. Sometimes we see it coming, other times we don't. Bad things can happen to anyone, anytime, anywhere. However, believing that these thoughts are done *to you* will trap you in a victim mentality. It distracts you from the truth, which is that these patterns of thought are simply a matter of habit. The trouble is most people tend to be too harsh on themselves. You're not trapped in prison; you're merely trapped in a bad habit. You see, the mind is like the needle of a compass. It can only point in a single direction at a time. This means that we're only meant to think and focus on *one thought at a time.* This fact is going to be the secret to successfully shifting your thoughts away from negativity because you *cannot* think of a negative *and* positive thought at the same time. One direction, one thought.

If you think of the mind as a compass needle, that means that the needle would have a magnetic north of its own. That magnetic north would default and point in the direction we are engaged in *out of habit.* If we predominantly have a history of negative thinking, such as when something happens to us and we don't like it, doing down a negative trail will only serve to strengthen this unhealthy habit we possess.

How do we change that and create a shift in our thoughts? Well, the body and the mind are both programmed to adapt to the environment that we are in. For example, when you look at your body and tell yourself, *"I have a big overweight body and I want to free myself from this,"* you know what the answer is. The key to freeing your body is to start a diet and exercise program that is right for you, stop putting the wrong type of things in your body, start putting the right things in, and take care of your body. Whether you put your body in a fast-food restaurant or a gym, it doesn't mind. It is going to adapt accordingly. Your mind works *exactly* the same way. By placing your mind in an environment where you're always *thinking* about negative thoughts since it is your default pattern, then that is what your mind is going to respond to. You keep building on these negative muscles, allowing them to grow stronger over time, and you'll be able to think stronger negative thoughts which have an even greater impact on your mental and emotional wellbeing.

The mind is also going to work if you work on strengthening the positive muscles too. *That's what you need to do.* To free yourself and create a shift in your thought patterns, focus on strengthening the positive mental muscles. To place your mind in a better environment. You need to consistently expose yourself, so your mind's compass needle gets a chance to point in a different direction. This is can only be accomplished over time. You can't walk into a gym with a body that is out of shape, spend an hour in there and walk out feeling fitter and stronger. It doesn't work that way for your body, and it doesn't work that way for your mind. You need to commit. Commit the time needed to take care of your mind and strengthen that positive muscle.

If you *don't make time* for positivity in your life, then your default mode is always going to swing toward the negative. You'll be unhappy and miserable for the rest of your life unless you do something right now to change that.

For most people, their default mode is negative. Their environment, their peers, their social media and most of the things they are associated with are constantly programming them toward the negative. That's why they find overcoming this to be such a struggle. To shift your thoughts, you need to start by making a conscious decision. That willpower and desire to create the shift is what drives your thoughts. So, make a firm and resolute decision that you are going to change your thoughts. How do you do that? With the following guidelines:

- Surround yourself with only the positive kind of individuals that are going to strengthen your mental muscles. Eliminate the toxic individuals in your life; they will do you no good.

- If you can't entirely eliminate the negative people in your environment, tune them out instead. Choose not to listen to them.

- Read inspirational books about other people who have overcome a great deal of hardship or struggle.

- Listen to positive podcast talks or watch positive films that make you feel uplifted and come from a place of positivity.

- Deliberately distract yourself so you have no time to dwell on what's keeping you in the negative zone.

- Push that negative thought back out. As soon as you notice its presence, commit 20 seconds to actively pushing that thought out of your mind.

- Surround your life with things and people that make you happy. You don't have to feel bad about removing negative or toxic people from your life if they weigh you down.

- Make time to do things that make you happy personally. Do it for yourself and no one else because it makes you feel good. Anything that you enjoy is always a good distraction from negativity.

- Choose to focus on what promotes happiness and let those elements be the ones that command your attention. Let them be in charge of your emotions.

- When negativity strikes, picture or visualize in your mind something that you are happy and grateful for. Think about the people you love, your pets, your friends, your passion, something you're looking forward to this weekend.

- Linger on the memory of past positive experiences until you feel a shift in your mood. When you feel negativity creeping in, channel your energy toward a positive memory and focus until you feel a perceptible shift in your mood.

- Identify who the positive people are in your life and choose to spend more time with them. Learn from them, emulate them and follow in their footsteps, doing everything that they do.

- As cheesy as it sounds, *smile* often. Your mind has the power to project happy thoughts from the actions you take. Happiness does not always have to come from the inside all the time. Persistent smiling activates endorphins and lowers your stress levels.

You can take charge of the environment you want to see yourself surrounded in. Nobody has the power to dictate what you should or should not do, say or think. *You are good enough* and you have *more potential* than you give yourself credit for. Everything that happens in your life is relative. It all depends on how you look at it.

Good Habits to Control Your Thoughts

Negative thoughts are something we all deal with all the time. There are so many different things that cause these negative thoughts; it's hard to keep track of them all. The one thing we do know for sure is that these thoughts must stop, or they are going to *stop you* from living your life. There are different things you can do to keep those negative thoughts from flooding your mind, one of which includes creating good habits that you stick to every day that protect you mentally and emotionally.

- **Habit #1: Realize How Lucky You Are** - If you've got a roof over your head, food in your belly, clothes, family, people who love and care about you, and a job that lets you pay the bills to afford the life you want, then you are lucky. No matter what else may be going on in your life, *you are lucky*. There are so many people out there who don't have half of the things you do, and they would trade places with you in a heartbeat given a chance. You've probably had more than your fair share of hearing how important it is to be grateful every day, but that's because it *cannot be emphasized enough*. It makes a tremendous difference to your mindset and it significantly diminishes the hold that negative thoughts have on you. Think about the people out there who live on the streets. People who don't have a place to call home. People who are all alone with no one to love them. No family, no friends. People who don't know where their next meal is coming from. What are negative thoughts compared to the struggles they have to go through, where each day feels like a battle just to stay alive or find the will to stay alive? You are so lucky and so blessed, and that fact alone squashes the power any negative thought has over your mind.

- **Habit #2: Habitually Seek the Silver Lining** - Before you rebuke this habit straight away and think it is too hard to do, resist the urge for a minute. Yes, you may wonder *"What do I have to be happy about when something bad happens? Where's the silver lining in that?"* but finding the silver lining doesn't mean that you need to necessarily be *happy* when something bad happens. It means you're trying to look for the good in these situations. Of course, you'll feel bad when something bad happens to you. That's the normal reaction and feeling unusually happy would be weird. Even when things are hard, there is *always* something good that you can find in *any* situation. There is always something that you can twist in the situation that makes you think *"Okay, I hate that this situation is happening, BUT on the positive side..."* It all depends on how you choose to look at it. There will be moments when something really terrible happens and you cannot find the silver lining no matter how hard you try. Admittedly, those might be some of the hardest times in your life. But if you look back and think about those challenging moments now, you'll see how much better and stronger you are because of what happened to you. That's the silver lining. It exists and it's always there. You only need to look hard enough for it.

- **Habit #3: Stop the Comparison** - The dark side of social media is how it brings out the worst in us at times. Specifically, in terms of the way we compare our lives to the lives of others we see on social media. There's an old saying that goes *"comparison is the thief of joy."* Oh, how true this is. The grass will always look greener on the other side if that is all you choose to focus on, and that's a habit a lot of people are guilty of in this day and age. You're comparing your life, your career, your friendships, your body image, and you're so busy Keeping Up with the Joneses you've forgotten to look at everything in life you have to be grateful for. A better habit that promotes keeping the negativity at bay would be to stay in your lane. Focus on *your* progression in life, not someone else's. Focus on all your blessings, not someone else's. The habit of putting a stop to comparison will leave you a *much* happier person. When you're happier, you keep negative thoughts out of your mind. It's hard, no doubt about it. Scrolling through any social media it is so easy to see how quickly you can be scooped up by negativity when you perceive other people "having it all" while you seem to struggle. Stay in your lane. It'll get you much further and make it easier to overcome your struggle with negativity.

- **Habit #4: Stop Playing the Victim** - There are people out there who go through life feeling like the world is always out to get them. Every day feels like a struggle for them. As soon as one small thing happens, they immediately think it happened because "people are out to get them" or the "universe is out to get them." Playing the victim (if that is a habit you currently have) is only going to leave you feeling stressed all the time. Not every bad thing that happens is happening *to you*. Sometimes it could be a blessing in disguise that is happening *for you*.

- **Habit #5: Name and Tame** - Name your thought to tame your thought. Be aware of your negative thoughts, because you cannot change what you're not aware of. It's as simple as that. Make it a new habit to acknowledge the thoughts that are going on in your mind instead of trying to run away from them. When a negative thought is happening, address it at that moment. Say to yourself *"This is a negative thought happening right now. This is my ancient brain's hardwiring at work."* Naming your negative thought is not going to immediately make the pain go away, but it will help to minimize the sting. As your positivity muscle strengthens with time, negative thoughts will start hurting a lot less too.

- **Habit #6: Intentional Attention Focus** - Deliberately learn where you want to focus on your attention. Ideally, you want to learn how to focus your attention on where it serves you best. This takes practice, and what you allow your mind to focus on will be the one that shapes your brain. If you make it a habit to deliberately choose to focus on something positive, that's what you're shaping and training your brain to focus more attention on. Instead of amplifying your pain by focusing on the negative, you're intentionally focusing your attention elsewhere.

- **Habit #7: Internalizing the Positive -** Your new habit is going to be internalizing anything positive that happens to you for at least 30 seconds. Focus so hard on that positive event that you're savoring every moment of it with all that you have. Your entire being, energy, and mind are so focused on it that for the next 30 seconds, this positive event consumes you. The best way to overcome your habit of leaning toward the negative is to embed as many positive experiences in your brain as possible. Even if that event seems small to you. For example, when you get a text from your friend thanking you for helping them through a problem yesterday. Instead of thinking *"That's nice"* and then forgetting all about it, spend at least 30 seconds soaking up the memory of how good it felt knowing that you helped that friend work through the issues they were having. What you're trying to do is cement that positivity in your brain

It does sound easier said than done, but that's the thing about habits. It's only difficult in the beginning. Once it *becomes your habit,* you'll go through the motions effortlessly without even having to push too hard. You always have the power in your hands to tip the scales in your favor. You don't have to stay on the negative side of the spectrum if you don't want to.

Chapter 5: Change Your Mind

The mindset that we carry around with us everyday matters. It matters in virtually every facet of our lives. Have you heard about the *placebo effect?* What is the true nature of the placebo effect anyway? Most people would assume that the placebo effect as nothing more than the way we respond to a faux pill or faux procedure. We believe the procedure, or the pill, has worked even though technically nothing has been done. That's *not* what the placebo effect is. The *true* nature of this effect is not about the fake pill or procedure, but rather it is a demonstration of just how powerful our mindsets can be.

Your mindset in literal terms is "the setting of your mind." Or rather, the way that your mind is set up. It is the lens or the frame of mind in which you view the world around you. Your mindset is the way you simplify the infinite number of possible ways to interpret the information that is coming at you each day. Simplifying the world with our mindsets is a natural part of the human cognitive process. It is the way that all of us make sense of the world. The way we process the information and how we use what we're learning to better our lives. Yet, despite the dramatic role they play in our ability to overcome negativity, not a lot of thought is given to this powerful force that resides within us. Instead, mindsets are treated as inconsequential and their true power gets dismissed too often.

Your mind is so powerful that it has the ability to shape the world around you. So powerful that you might not even notice the placebo effect taking place. Take exercise for example. When you spend all that time committed to working out and training your body, is your body getting stronger *because of* the time you spend training it? Or is your body getting stronger *because you expect it to?* That's a very interesting concept that was put forth by Dr. Alia Crum in one of her TedX Talks. This gets you thinking about mindsets and how they matter.

Take stress for example. What do you think about stress? Well, if you're like most people out there, then stress probably has negative connotations associated with it in your mind. You hear the word "stress" and you immediately think, "bad!" Not surprising, since everything you hear and see about stress acts as a warning label, reminding you of how harmful it is to your health. But as we know, it's not as black and white as that. Stress is the body's natural response mechanism; we know that. But what we don't pay attention to is the fact that stress *can be good for you,* and there's no shortage of evidence supporting this either. Stress in the right doses could spur you to perform better, motivate you to accomplish more, and give you the push you need to excel at what you do. It all depends on how you look at it.

If you could shift your mind, change and alter it to become more beneficial to you, would you do it? Absolutely.

What Exactly Are Bad Habits?

Essentially, it is an ingrained pattern of behavior. Once a habit has become so deeply rooted and ingrained in you, it becomes even more difficult to break out of. A *bad habit* is defined as any habit that stands in the way of you achieving your long-term goals. These bad habits tend to stick around for two reasons:

- They are ingrained in us

- They almost always lead to short-term goals

Since the brain is hardwired to care more about the short-term goals and anything that brings immediate benefit to satisfy its need for instant gratification, negative bad habits usually win out at the end of the day. Logically, you know your long-term goals are more important. But it's difficult to remind your brain of that. To break out of these mental bad habits, you need a reason that is well-defined, clear and compelling enough.

Martial artist Bruce Lee once penned in one of his many private journals this thought: *"I realize that my mind's dominating thoughts will eventually reproduce in outwards, physical action that will gradually transform and become my physical reality. Therefore, I will choose to concentrate my thoughts daily for 30 minutes. I will think about the person I intend to become and create a clear mental picture in my mind."* For Lee, that reason was compelling enough to give him the focus he needed to gain control of his mind. To change your mind, you need to find *your* compelling reason.

How to Bring About A Shift in Your Mind

Samuel Thomas Davies, a writer, said this about self-discipline which sums up what it is in a tidy way:

"Self-discipline means leaning into resistance. To take action regardless of how you feel. To purposely live your life by design and not by default. But most important of all, self-discipline means you act based on your THOUGHTS, not your feelings."

Bringing about a mental shift in your mind toward becoming a more disciplined, mentally resilient individual boils down to how willing you are to do it regardless of the way you feel. To be able to push forward even when you don't want to. That's self-discipline. Bringing about a shift in your mindset is possible if you take that challenge seriously. You can't say *I want to change* and then forget about it 5-minutes later. You need to be serious about that challenge to change or it is never going to happen.

To begin creating this mental shift, you need to follow these guidelines as best you can:

- **If You're Going to Be the Worst Person in the Room, Be Okay with It** - This would probably make a lot of people flinch. Why on earth would we want to be okay with being the *worst* person in the room? Don't we want to be the best? *Shouldn't we be* the best? The fear of being labeled as "the worst" or the fear of looking bad in comparison to others will always keep you from pursuing the things you want to do. Without changing your mind and changing this fear, you're always going to feel "stuck." This fear will always keep you from pushing your limits and improving. But the moment you change your mindset and start to be okay with the idea of being "the worst" at what you do, you'll automatically change gears and start working on improving. Think about it. If you really are "the worst," then logically, there's nowhere else for you to go but up. Everyone else around you are people you can learn from and making the switch to this mindset alone immediately makes you see things in a whole different light.

- **Be Okay with Making Mistakes** - A lot of the time, we put unnecessary pressure on ourselves to get things right the first time. When we make a mistake, we immediately start to feel defeated and be too hard on ourselves. That's not how things are supposed to be. You're *supposed* to make mistakes because it's part of the learning process. When you start seeing your mistakes as part of the learning process, you open your mind to *undergoing* that learning process. You stop being too hard on yourself, and you feel significantly less stressed when you take away the pressure of trying to get it perfect right away.

- **Similar Replacements** - Breaking out of bad habits is tough because of the constant craving to give in to temptation. Therefore, what you need to do is find a similar replacement that is going to give you that same kind of reward. This will encourage the shift toward a habit that is more productive, eventually getting rid of the bad habit you've been carrying around gradually. This is going to require some digging into your thoughts to find what the actual reward is that you crave. If you're repeatedly engaging in a habit knowing that it is bad for you anyway, there must be a reason why. Once you find that reason, think about something similar (but better) that could give you the same benefits.

- **Remove Access to Negativity -** If you have no access to negativity, you won't be able to give in to temptation. When there's nothing to tempt you, there's nothing to lead you off track. By removing the access you have to negativity, you're already giving your mind the leverage it needs to hold on to the positive thoughts it has been practicing so far. Negativity will always hold you back unless you start to minimize the access you have to it.

- **Challenge Yourself for 30-Days-** If you're struggling with getting started in trying to create a shift in your mindset, try challenging yourself to stick to this new routine for at least 30-days. Going against something that has felt natural to you for so long is not going to be easy. Challenging yourself for 30 days sounds difficult when you think about it, but anyone can do it. *Anyone.* The key is to make yourself accountable for your actions. When you're accountable, you're invested in your success.

- **Think About Your Legacy -** What do you want your legacy to be? To create that positive shift in your mind, think about what you want your legacy to be. What impression do you want to leave behind for your family? Do you want them to remember you as someone who was stressed all the time? Someone who had difficulty coping? Would you want your children or other members of your family picking up on the negative mindsets you have? Loved ones can be an immensely powerful and motivating factor to bring about the change you need. After all, what better reason to change for the better than to do it for the people you love.

- **Think About Your Rut -** It's not enough to say *"I'm stuck in a rut"* when you're thinking about changing your mindset. That is a generality, and if you're going to fix a problem, you need the details and the specifics of what it is you're trying to fix. Where are you stuck in a rut at? Your relationships? Finances? Career? Why are you stuck and why is it not working anymore? Get into the specifics of it. Shift your mindset by identifying where you want to be in that *specific* area. For example, if you say you're stuck in a rut career-wise, identify where you want to be in that area. Where are you now in that area and how to do you get there? Don't worry about what other people are doing. Focus on you and what you're doing.

- **Be Okay with Confronting Bad News -** People would naturally prefer to avoid bad news. They would rather avoid looking at the harsh realities that they have to face. Unfortunately, this approach tends to cause a lot of problems. In your attempt to avoid pain, you might resort to avoiding confrontation with what you know is going to cause you mental pain. However, truly successful individuals are the ones who are strong enough to confront these harsh and challenging realities. Once you're able to do so and get over the emotional pain they cause, your brain then begins to formulate ways to overcome this negativity. You'll never really get used to seeing bad news or hearing bad news, but you can change the way you perceive them, so it doesn't have to impact you as strongly.

Until your mindset changes, everything else in your life is going to stay the same. You need to change your mindset *first* before you can start seeing real change in your life. You could change your lifestyle and *still* find yourself slipping back into your old habits. You change your jobs, change where you live, change your relationships, but all the while maintaining the same mindset. That's why you're not moving forward. You're not focused on changing the right thing yet.

Good Habits to Control Your Mind

When you say that you're grateful, you need to *mean it*. Don't say it for the sake of doing so, but you need to believe it if you want your mind to believe it wholeheartedly too. Everyone has the capability within them to build good mental habits to control your mind. Bad habits will cost you your happiness, so why indulge in them any longer than you have to? Why continue to indulge in the habits that lead to unhappiness and misery when you could choose to exert that same energy toward building good habits that help you better control your mind?

Saying that you "can't help the way you think" only leads to the belief that you don't have any power at all. But you *do* and it's time that you started actively doing something about it. Sticking with your old mental habits is only eating away at your mental strength. There are certain destructive beliefs that make us less effective and deprive us of the mental strength we need to initiate change in our lives. One such destructive belief is what we think about ourselves. We're prone to feeling sorry for ourselves. It is okay to be sad at times when bad things happen; self-pity is more than that. When you begin to magnify the misfortune in your mind, you're no longer in control. You're relinquishing control to your negative thoughts, and *that's why* it feels so hard to try and overcome them.

What you need are good habits. Habits that will help you take control of your mind. Habits that allow you to remain in the driver seat at all times, no matter what happens to you, good or bad. Good habits that don't leave you feeling stuck or focused on the problem. Habits that lead to you taking steps to make your life better. It's hard to get rid of negative mental habits and unhealthy beliefs that you've carried around with you for so long. But giving them up is something you must do. Sooner or later, you're going to reach a time in your life where you need all the mental strength you can muster to control your mind. When you're going through really bad periods in your life, good habits might not seem like they are enough to get you through the storm. It only takes one or two small negative habits to hold you back.

Get rid of these bad habits by replacing them with these good ones instead:

- **Habit #1: Feel Comfortable with Your Feelings -** A lot of the bad mental habits we have happen when we're uncomfortable with the emotions we feel. The negative, self-deprecating thoughts you have about yourself happen when you're uncomfortable with the emotions you feel. Feeling scared, anxious, sad, fearful, angry, all these emotions are uncomfortable. Therefore, you find yourself going to great lengths to try and avoid that discomfort. You try to escape those feelings by indulging in bad habits like feeling sorry for yourself or adopting the victim mentality. The only way to deal with your uncomfortable emotions is to go through them. To be comfortable enough to let them in, experience them, and then move forward.

- **Habit #2: Accept That You Are Unique -** You are unique with a personality of your own. You're not like your friend, your relative, your neighbor or your colleague. You are *you,* and that is a wonderful thing to be. By embracing this notion wholeheartedly, you remain in control of your mind. Negative thoughts no longer have the power to creep in and destroy your confidence and belief in yourself because you've accepted who you are. If you have to compare, compare yourself to the person you were yesterday. Look at how you have improved since then and think about all that you could be in the future.

- **Habit #3: Give Up Wanting the World to Be Fair -** It's never going to be fair. It's easy to be happy and cheerful when everything is going your way. As soon as *one* bad thing happens, you break down and start to wonder *why me?* or *why does this happen to me?* Putting enough good deeds out there in the world hoping nothing bad will ever happen to you is only setting yourself up for disappointment. A good mental habit you need to adopt right now is the acceptance that life is not fair. That's the way it has always been. Yes, it means you're not necessarily always going to be rewarded for the good deeds you do, but it also means that when bad things happen; you're not going to suffer forever.

- **Habit #4: Focusing on Your Identity -** When you're trying to change your behavior, you need to *forget* about what goal you're trying to achieve. Forget about the external outcome and focus instead on changing your *identity*. Imagine if there were two people sitting at the same table, trying to resist the temptation to eat a plate of cookies placed in front of them. When offered a cookie, Person A says no thank you because they are trying to lose some weight and watch what they eat. Despite what Person A says, they are still tempted to indulge in the cookie and satisfy their sweet tooth. By resisting that cookie, Person A is trying to be someone they are not. Secretly they want the cookie, but they're telling themselves they don't. Person B, on the other hand, rejects the cookies and says no thank you, I don't have a sweet tooth. There's a small difference between the two statements, but the difference signals a shift in identity. Person B is going to be more successful because they know their identity, which is not having a sweet tooth, and they act in alignment with that. One your brain has decided to take a stand, you're going to encounter pressure to behave consistently with that belief. Think of your identity as someone who successfully overcame your negativity mindset and that shift in your mindset will do wonders in helping you stick to your good mental habits. Start thinking about the identity you want to embody. That'll bring about the changes you want to see.

- **Habit #5: Set Reminders-** Remind yourself *why* you're building these habits that will strengthen the control you have over your mind. At the end of the day, you must have a strong enough reason *why* for your actions is you want to be consistent with them until it becomes an automatic habit. Write down your goal or the identity you want for yourself and carry those reminders around with you. Each time you find yourself struggling, use those reminders to recall why you're fighting this hard to develop better mental habits. These reasons why give you the push you need to keep moving forward when everything else is trying to persuade you to give up.

- **Habit #6: Target Your Fundamentals -** Sleep, nutrition, exercise, hydration. Those are some of the basic life fundamentals you need to perform at your best each day. The area of your brain that handles executive functioning and regulates your impulses and desires is going to need a lot of energy and regular rest to pull it off successfully. When you're not taking care of the fundamental basics you need to be in peak mental and physical health, you're not going to be able to focus enough to develop the mental strength and resilience you need. You're not going to be able to focus long enough to bring about the desired change you want. The brain is not a machine that can keep going. It needs rest and it needs exercise too. It needs to be well looked after. Take care of your fundamentals first and give your brain the fuel it needs so it can go full steam ahead.

Being in control of your mind and developing the mental strength you need to be resilient requires both cultivating good habits and giving up the bad ones you've been carrying around with you. No matter how small these negative habits seem to be. You can practice gratitude (good habit) when you simultaneously resent someone else's good fortune (bad habit). Your world is what you make it, and you *can* make it a world where you've developed enough mental strength, resilience and good mental habits to remain calm and in control always.

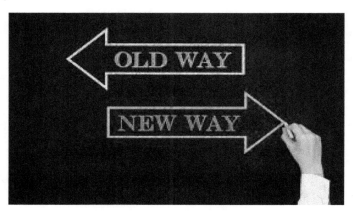

Chapter 6: Paradigm Shift

What do you want to do? How often have you asked yourself that question? If you're struggling to overcome anxiety, then it's probably not often enough. The truth of the matter is, the only limitations we have are the ones we impose on ourselves. If you think you *can't do something,* you won't do it. If you think *you can,* you'll go to any lengths to try and make it happen. When the motivation and belief in yourself are there, anything is possible.

There are no limitations. None. it is your belief that is holding you back and creating this perceived limit. If we thought about all the beliefs we had right now and made a list, we would realize that most of these beliefs are absurd. Yet, these limiting beliefs get passed on from one generation to the next. If you grew up in a family that believed starting a business was risky and doomed for failure, then that limiting belief would stop us from ever chasing after any entrepreneurship dreams we may have. The limitations we carry around are often influenced by someone else's rules. The rules that they made based on what they believed in that cause us to doubt our abilities. They cause us to question if we can do something, and the more we dwell on the hesitation, the harder it becomes to act on it.

What Is A Paradigm?

The term "paradigm" is a term used in psychology that denotes *mindset*. In short, it is the way you view and see things. Think of a paradigm as a pair of eyeglasses. If you were to put on a pair of glasses that had a red-tinted lens on it, what do you think the world would look like to you? Obviously, the world would take on a "rosy tint" because of the lens through which you're viewing it. Those red-tinted lenses are altering what you're seeing. If you switched the red lenses for some green ones instead, what would happen then? The world starts looking a little green, doesn't it? Let's say you were looking at your pet through the red lenses first and now you're looking at the same pet but through green lenses. One moment your pet has a red tint to them, and the next they're "green-ish."

Did the world change? Did your pet change? No, they didn't. But the way *you saw it changed*. It changed because of the lenses that you put on. That's how paradigm works too.

An interesting experiment was conducted back in the 1800s by a psychologist by the name of George M. Stratton. In this experiment, Stratton designed a pair of eyeglasses that turned everything he saw upside down. Stratton had a hard time finding subjects to sign up for his study because they thought he was nuts. Why would anyone want to see the world upside down? Since Stratton couldn't find any willing volunteers, he decided to put the eyeglasses on himself. Initially, he had a hard time adjusting to his surroundings. He was bumping into things and struggling to move around since his perception was distorted. But after a couple of hours, he started adjusting to it. After several days, he started getting used to moving around better despite his surroundings looking like they were upside down. Stratton persisted with his experiment and by the 8th day, *everything started to look normal to him.* That point amazed him the most. Upon taking off the glasses, the "real" world looked distorted to him and he had to adjust his mindset back again before everything went back to normal. His mind did *exactly* what everyone else's mind is capable of doing. It corrects the images that you see so that they start to appear "normal." Bear in mind, though, that what looks normal to you might not look the same to someone else.

We are already getting this same experience with the sunglasses we wear, believe it or not. Sure, the world doesn't look upside down when we put them on, but when you do put them on, the world around you looks a little darker. *At first.* After a couple of hours wearing them? Doesn't everything start to look normal that you don't even notice your sunglasses anymore? It does not mean the world looks that way, but it means the world *looks normal to you because that is what you're used to.* This is how paradigms work.

Paradigms are set up in our minds through the experiences we go through. These experiences give us a certain way of viewing the world. Paradigms boil down to two determinant and distinct sides, and we usually find ourselves on one side or the other. The first side is **the victim (negative)** and the second side is **the agent (positive).** In the "Victim" paradigm, you put on a "victim" pair of eyeglasses. This means you start to adopt a "victim" way of seeing the world (the victim mentality). Through these glasses, you believe that the world is out to get you; everything always happens to you. The problem always lies outward and you don't think about looking inward for a source and solution. A "victim" will go through their entire lives blaming someone else or something else for where they are in life. No surprise why this paradigm sits on the negative end. As long as you keep blaming something or someone else for what's going on in your life, you will never have the power to change it. As long as you keep blaming, your mind will never have enough power or resources to overcome negativity.

Now, if you went the other way and looked at the "Agent" paradigm, there is a stark difference. An "agent" who straps on a pair of "agent" lenses takes responsibility because of the paradigm through which they are now viewing the world. Unlike the other paradigm, this one puts you in charge. You get to be the one who is in the driver's seat, steering the direction you want your life to go in. Just like what you would do if you were driving, if you don't like where you are, steer your life in a different direction. It really is that simple. It takes effort, but the effort is *manageable*. Thinking that you "can't do it" is a false limiting belief that once again, you're imposing on yourself. The "Agent' paradigm gives you that power to change, something victims can't do because they're too busy focused on blaming someone or something else. The right kind of paradigm has the power to exact the change you want to see.

Putting on the "Agent" lenses is empowering. Instead of saying *"Why me?"* you start asking *"Why NOT me?"* You're just as qualified as anyone else to take on the challenges that make you stronger. You're just as capable as anyone else to take on new opportunities that get thrown your way. You're just as strong and resilient as anyone else and if they can do it, *why not you?* See how much more empowering that kind of thinking is? By simply putting on a different pair of lenses over your eyes, your perspective and way of thinking immediately change. That's why the limits that we *think we have* are actually nonexistent. The word *"I can't"* is like a big switch in your brain. As soon as you hit that switch, your brain immediately shuts down. You stop thinking of solutions, you stop trying to figure things out, you just stop trying altogether. You hold yourself back by uttering those two, simple, powerful words. As opposed to when you say *"I can! How do I do it?"* You're turning your mental switch back on when you say that phrase and right away your mindset changes. Your brain is now actively working to find the resources you need that will allow you to solve any problem you're facing. *Any* problem.

The "Victim" paradigm also puts you in a state of scarcity. This mindset will lead to the limiting belief that nothing is ever enough. That you don't have enough time, energy, money, love, attention, or anything else for that matter. No matter what, it will feel like it is never enough. Unfortunately, the scarcity mindset is an easy one to slip into without noticing. It starts from the first thought you have the moment you wake up. Wake up thinking *"I didn't get enough sleep last night"* and you've already put yourself on the scarcity paradigm. See how quickly it can happen? The shift you are going to try and create right now is a shift toward the "Agent" side. A state of mind where abundance rules instead of scarcity. With abundance, there's *always* enough. Enough time, enough energy, you've got enough to do everything you want and more. The choice of which paradigm side you end up on comes down to you. You may not always get to choose *what* happens to you, but you *can* choose your paradigm. Always.

Let's go back to the Stratton experiment for a minute. If you put on the pair of eyeglasses that were tinted red and the world around you looks red, that's not going to look entirely right, is it? We know the world around us is not red all the time. When it's not something you're used to, it doesn't feel right. But what we can take away from the Stratton experiment is that we *can get used* to it. It's not going to feel right or look good because you're not accustomed to it, but you *will* get used to it just like how Stratton got used to seeing his world upside down. It's easy to reject what feels unfamiliar and that's the first obstacle you're going to have to overcome to shift your paradigm. Don't discount or reject a new paradigm right away. Fight against that instinct to reject what feels unfamiliar. If you keep practicing and pushing toward a shift in your paradigm, eventually, it is going to look normal to you. You might need to persist long enough until you get it.

How to Bring About A Shift in Your Paradigm

We are programmed in two ways:

- Genetically

- Environmentally

This is part of your paradigm. You do have the ability to create a shift in this paradigm. To shape your future, you need to be willing to change your paradigm. Most people might be willing to change, but they're not *able* to initiate this change because they don't fully understand what they need to do. If your paradigm is causing you enormous problems, it is evident that something needs to change. If everything that is happening in your life right now is *not* what you want, then it's time to create that shift in your paradigm. Most people go through life never being truly happy, not realizing that a lot of their unhappiness is motivated by the paradigms they choose or allow themselves to live in. You can try to change a lot of things in your life, but if you find you keep falling back into old habits and ways of thinking, that can only mean one thing. *You're not changing yourself from within (paradigm).*

Your paradigm is your subconscious conditioning. They are nothing more than a group of habits. These habits have been programmed into your subconscious mind and it controls your behavior. Your behavior *causes* your results, and if you want to change your results, look within. There are certain things you need to do to bring about a shift in your paradigm, and it often comes down to simply changing the way you see the world:

- **Feeding Your Mind with Goodness** - Your mind absorbs what you tell it. Feed it with negativity and that will become the paradigm that you live in. Feed it positivity and watch your entire life start to change. It sounds like a made-up cliché until you try it. You are the guardian of your mind. You decide what gets put into your mind each day. That choice will always reside with you. Each morning when you wake up, choose to feed your mind with something positive and nurturing. An inspirational passage from a book. An affirming quote. An empowering podcast, even. Just 30-minutes of your time every day when you're feeding your mind with something good, you're strengthening it. When you do a physical workout that gets your heart pumping and the blood flowing, instantly your biochemistry changes. From feeling uninspired and reluctant before the workout, once you've completed it, you feel so much better. Accomplished and motivated even. You think *"Wow! I'm glad I did that after all."* It works the same way with your mind.

- **There's Always Someone Worse Off Than You Are** - We often don't realize how good we have it in life until we meet someone who has it worse off than we do. There's an old saying: *I once cried because I had no shoes until I met a man who had no feet.* That's a fault we're all guilty of. We spend far too much time focusing on what's lacking and what is going wrong in our lives that we forget we have a lot to be grateful for. A shift in your paradigm happens with the simple act of spending time helping someone who is worse off than you are. It reminds you that there is a lot more to life than the immediate problems we are dealing with.

- **Find A Mission Bigger Than Yourself** - It gives your mind something else to fixate on rather than the negative things that might be happening to you right now. Everyone has got good and bad moments happening in their day, their week, month, and life. The difference is how you choose to let those negative elements impact you. It's easy to get fixated on the bad and lose sight of the good if you don't have something concrete to focus on. So, find a mission or a goal that is bigger than yourself and hold onto that.

- **Find A Role Model -** Someone you can look up to and emulate because they embody all the qualities that you hope to one day see in yourself. Having a role model makes it "real." These are real people who showed that change is possible. They are a role model of everything that is possible if you tried.

Good Habits to Control Your Paradigm

Paradigm. The blueprint of how you view your life. Your beliefs that contribute to your perception. The experiences that have shaped you to become the person you are today. Those elements are part of your paradigm. Once you've established that you want to create a shift in your paradigm using the techniques above, there's another thing you've got to do to ensure you don't fall right back to your unhealthy habits: *Establishing good habits to control your paradigm.*

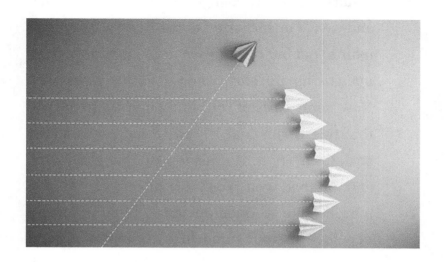

- **Habit #1: Start with Results You Want to Change** - The biggest changes can be brought about by changing the smallest habits. Let's say you want to start getting up earlier in the morning so you can get more done during the day. That's a simple enough result to create. To bring about the change, look at what is causing you to sleep in and wake up late each morning. What is it that keeps you hitting the snooze button even when you know you shouldn't? Pinpoint the exact negative results you're getting, for example, *"I'm always hitting the snooze button, I never wake up early, I'm not disciplined enough."* Write all that down, and then look at what the polar opposite of those

113

results are. Now, change the way you view that and say, *"I'm energized when I wake up, I can't wait to get out of bed each day, I get more done by waking up early than I ever did before!"* Now, some parts of your brain may try to tell you that this is silly and it's not going to work. But stick to it. Try it. Do this for 30 days and by the end of that, you won't be hitting the snooze button quite so often anymore. Programming a new idea in your mind takes time, but once it sticks, it takes over and your old negative habit starts to die out because you're not feeding it anymore.

- **Habit #2: Learn to Pause -** This habit works along the same premise as learning to say "no" when you need to. You've got a lot of powerful and positive empowering beliefs that you're carrying around with you. At the same time, you've got a lot of "junk" or "unhelpful" thoughts in there too that could be affecting your perception. When you feel too overwhelmed by a thought or emotion, or when something feels too negative, learn to pause. Pause and learn to identify that your *thoughts* are the ones

114

responsible for creating what you feel and what you see. It's not necessarily your reality. It can be confusing when you look around at everything that's going on. When you look at the evidence you're surrounded with, your mind tells you that it *has to be true*. But everything that you're feeling and thinking is always *optional*. If it wasn't optional, then everyone would be experiencing and feeling the same thing you are. But they don't. Two people could go through the same experience and both would see it from very different perspectives. Learn to pause. Give yourself time to process the information you're receiving and remember it does not necessarily have to equal your reality.

- **Habit #3: Question Your Limits -** What is your biggest limiting thought that is stopping you from going after what you want right now? If you had to do something and your first thought is *"I can't,"* why is that? Tune out all the distractions, the emails, the conversations, the texts, the social media notifications and just stop. Allow your mind a few minutes of quiet calm as you begin searching for the answer.

Close your eyes, breathe, feel grounded. Now think about what's your biggest limiting belief at the moment? What evidence do you have to support that? Is that belief serving you? If it isn't, why do you continue to hold onto it? Now, ask what beliefs would serve you better? For example, if your limiting belief is not being able to work mobile or while you're traveling, what solutions could you come up with that would better serve you? Find solutions or ideas that you like a lot more than your limiting belief and make it a new habit to replace those negative thoughts with effective solutions that make you feel good.

- **Habit #4: Attaching Emotion** - Your emotions are what anchor your thoughts. When something happens that makes you feel angry, the emotions that accompany that episode contributes to the way that you feel. In fact, that angry emotion might hold you in place and stop you from moving past what happened. That's why you find yourself feeling angry for hours, days, weeks or even months. It also happens to be the reason why so many people have trouble letting go of anger and grudges. The emotions that accompany your thoughts and experiences are an anchor and they will keep you trapped in that paradigm. A new habit you're going to adopt in this paradigm shift is to begin attaching emotions to the positive thoughts you want to nourish. The same thing is happening, but this time you're shifting the focus from negative to positive. Visualize the result that you want to see happening and focus your energy on that. If you're visualizing yourself achieving success at work, imagine all the emotions that are going to accompany that moment. Feel the happiness and joy at seeing your hard work pay off. Attach that emotion to it each time you visualize until you find yourself taking action steps to turn your vision into reality.

- **Habit #5: Doing Things Differently -** Your paradigms are your habits; therefore, it makes sense that to bring about the changes you see, you need to do things *differently* from what you did before. What do you get to do differently that is the polar opposite of the bad habit you're trying to break? Go back to the earlier example of wanting to wake up earlier in the morning. Your action step was to approach the problem of not being able to wake up early was to change the way you viewed that habit by telling yourself how energized and excited you are to seize the day. Breaking out of old habits doesn't have to involve a major overhaul. Sometimes all it takes is a small tweak in an old habit to set you on a completely different path.

Chapter 7: Improve Your Life

Overcoming negativity is an uphill battle. When it wraps its finger around you, it can quickly seep into every area of your life. All it takes is one negative thought and before you know it, you find yourself dealing with depression, wondering how your life got to this point. It's a harsh reality. Negativity is always going to find a way to stay in your life unless you forcibly push it out of your life. Difficult times in life will always be a factor. That's a part of life and it is meant to test your willpower and endurance to keep fighting and surviving. Everything you have gone through is meant to make you stronger and better, but sometimes negativity can be a huge morale blow, and many find themselves quickly losing heart when the road looks rough ahead.

Overcoming negativity is hard; there's no doubt about that. It's unfortunate that negativity seems to be the stronger superpower. But every superpower has a weakness, and that's your good news.

Importance of Self-Discipline

Self-discipline and willpower are two of the greatest assets you can possess to overcome negativity and improve your life once and for all. Especially today when it is becoming increasingly more difficult to maintain self-discipline. Why does self-discipline and willpower matter? Let's look at this example:

Think about a time when you've been tempted to do something that you later regret or feel guilty about. How often have you wished you could take it back? Or if given a chance, you would choose not to do it.

Moments like these are often a result of a lapse of judgment or a lack of discipline. Your ability to discipline your actions and your mind is an important skill to develop as part of your journey to overcome negativity. It also happens to be one of the *hardest* skills to master when you're just starting out, mostly because we live in a world that is filled with distraction and temptation. But when you learn to master the art of self-discipline and willpower, any feasible dream that you have becomes an objective, separated from you only by time. Even the longest and most impossible journey (like trying to overcome the negativity that has plagued you for so long) can be achieved if you persist.

When you continue to put one foot in front of the other, the only thing that will stop you from reaching that finish line is a lack of willpower and desire.

Self-discipline is a tough skill to master, and it might take you longer than expected to get there. It could even be much harder than you expected it to be. What you need is an effective blueprint that serves as your guide, like the steps listed below.

- **Define A Goal That Is Worth It -** When you have a goal that you want so badly, you're willing to do just about anything to make it happen. That's a goal you think is worth fighting for. For this step to work, the goal has to come from a place of deep desire within you. This step is not going to work on every goal because not all goals are equal. A goal that is worth fighting for is defined as a goal that is going to dramatically change your life when it happens. Like making your first million dollars or overcoming negativity to reclaim the happiness you thought was long lost. A goal that is worth fighting for is a goal that gives you goosebumps and sends a shiver down your spine when you think about it. It makes you say, *"I want this!"* This goal needs to be strong enough to get you through the toughest times (and there will be a lot of tough times to prepare for). A goal that is worth fighting for is your lighthouse in the distance. When you feel at a loss or ready to give up, follow the light to remind you that you're not that far away if you don't give up. Find the right goal and nothing will stand in your way, not even the negative thoughts that threaten to jeopardize everything you've worked so hard for.

- **Deconstructing Your Goal** - Finding that goal worth fighting for was the easy part. What you need to do now is analyze that goal and break it apart. Deconstruct it. Without the deconstruction process, it's not a goal anymore. It's a wish. Any goal that you have can be broken down into smaller pieces to make that goal easier to analyze. When you put all these deconstructed pieces together, they should fit perfectly to form the bigger picture. You need to identify what are the necessary ingredients needed for your goal to work. For example, to overcome negativity. What elements are needed to make that goal happen? How would you deconstruct this overall goal? The answers will be highly subjected, based on the individual and the outcome they want to achieve. Going back to the goal of overcoming negativity, the ingredients you'll need to make that goal happen might include a list of inspirational podcasts to listen to each day, sourcing these podcasts, allocating a time of day when you will commit to listening to these podcasts and how long that will take, and what your purpose is for listening to these podcasts. Deconstructing the goal is meant to give you a better understanding of *why* you're doing what you do, which makes it a lot more likely you're going to see the task all the way through.

- **Removing Distractions and Temptations -** An obvious step to take would be to distance and separate yourself from the very things that are causing you to get distracted and deviate away from your goal. There will always be a part of your brain that is aware of your environment, no matter how hard you try to concentrate on the task at hand. Especially if the distraction happens to be negative since our brains are already hardwired to be attracted to negativity.

What you can do to increase your discipline is to take control of your environment and removing any and all forms of distraction is one way to go about it. If your goal is to overcome negativity, remove distractions like social media and limit the time you spend around toxic people who will distract you from your goal.

- **Don't Wait for the "Right" Time -** There will never be a "right" or "perfect" time to start working on your self-discipline. If you want to work on becoming better, you need to work now and keep working until you make it happen. Overcoming negativity requires constant effort, and constant effort takes a lot of discipline and willpower. Waiting for the right time is merely postponing the evitable. Whether you begin today, tomorrow, or next week, the process is still going to be the same. The time and commitment needed are going to be the same. There is no such thing as waiting for the "right" time in this case. The best time to start improving your self-discipline will always be *right now*. If you only put in the work "when you feel like it," you'll never reap the rewards you hope to see.

- **Schedule Breaks and Little Rewards -** There's a difference between resting and quitting. We're only human and we're bound to get tired after a while. Pushing yourself to become better than you were yesterday is hard work, and when you're tired, it's okay to take a break to recharge your batteries. Learning to take breaks instead of quitting could change the way you view the tasks you take on from this point forward. Most of us believe we need to keep pushing, pushing and pushing until we finish what we started to do. Despite the tiredness, they just keep pushing and then give in to the temptation to quit when the body and mind burn out. Your body and your mind are not machines. They need fuel and you need to recharge. This is part of shifting your paradigm, changing the way you view accomplishing your goals. Reaching goals is a marathon, not a sprint and if you feel like a short break or little treat along the way, take it if it's going to renew your motivation. Reward yourself when you've overcome a particularly difficult challenge. You've earned it. The rewards should be little parts of what the big goal will feel like. This will strengthen your discipline and motivation to keep going.

- **Tracking Your Progress** - Measuring your progress gives you a clear understanding of your situation. Without measurable results, you wouldn't know which areas of your plan needed improvements. Yes, even overcoming negativity needs measurable results you can track. Everything that *can* be measured *should* be measured. This is how you will uncover which steps work and separate them from the ones that don't. This type of information allows you to make educated decisions for any goal you set for yourself. This way, you're not blindly shooting in the dark hoping that you'll get lucky. It's reassuring to see that the effort you're putting in is actually yielding measurable results. The small wins will serve as a reminder to keep the discipline going when you begin to see real changes in your life.

There is no elevator to get to the life you want. If there were, everyone would be living their best life and in an ideal world, no one would be struggling with negativity, worries, anxieties and all the other conditions that strip away the happiness we feel. Self-discipline is about finding ways to diminish the impact that negative thinking and habits have on your life. To get to where you want to be, you need to take the stairs. The progress is slower, but the final outcome will be well worth it.

Master Your Mind, Boost Your Brain

Your mind is your worst enemy. Every time you struggle, every time you feel like you fall short, every time you succumb to the power of negativity, that's your mind being in control. It is what's happening within your mind more so than anything happening in your external environment that gets in your way. Yet, we don't realize this because of how distracting the external stimuli can be. When you're about to get on stage and give a speech, for example, it's not the audience or being in the spotlight with all eyes on you that is the biggest problem. It is the *thoughts* in your mind that are making you feel nervous, anxious, and visualize all sorts of negative scenarios. It is your mind that is getting you all worked up and you think, *"I can't do this!"*

If you could master your mind and get these thoughts to *work with you* rather than against you, you're going to find that every goal you set for yourself is downhill from there. The negativity we experience is because our mind, brain, and entire nervous system are trying its best to protect us from what it perceives as pain. The negativity and anxiety that you feel is your mind's attempt to keep you away from what it thinks will be causing you pain. One of the biggest reasons why so many of us fail to become the masters of our mind is because we *don't understand* the way the subconscious mind works.

Our true power comes from deep within the subconscious mind, which is different from the role the conscious mind has. If your intention is to attract or change something about yourself, in this case learning how to master your mind, you need to utilize the subconscious mind's potential.

- **Think About the Pain of *Not* Changing** - If you think dealing with negativity is bad, imagine how much harder, more miserable and more painful your life would be if you *didn't* make an effort to change. If living like this is already making you miserable, what's going to happen when you have to spend the rest of your life like this? To spend your entire life thinking negatively, always stagnant and never moving forward because your mindset is not changing? That sounds a lot worse, doesn't it? Therefore, the short-term pain of training yourself to be disciplined enough to carry out all the steps needed to overcome the negativity that you've read about in this book doesn't seem so bad after all.

- **Think About the Cost of Staying Negative -** If you allowed your mind to continue to be the one in control, what is that going to cost you? Living with negativity, for instance, might cost you your career, relationships, friendships, a chance at love, or even going after your dreams. That's the cost of not becoming the master of your mind. To feel like you're never the one in control could end up costing you a lot of things in your life. Is it worth it? Probably not.

- **Be Willing to Take Risks** - Ask yourself *"What's the worst that could happen?"* There are thousands if not millions of people out there who are pushing and stretching past their comfort zones every day. What's the worst that could happen? When their mind is trying to tempt them to say "no" or "don't do it, they push back against that and do it anyway. What's the worst that could happen? Maybe you fall short or the risk doesn't quite pan out the way you hoped, but would it really be so bad? Complacency is the enemy of future possibilities and an invitation for negativity to settle in your mind. If you want a better life, you need to challenge your subconscious mind for control. Seek out new ways to push your boundaries; you'll become a stronger and wiser person in the process.

- **Great Expectations** - They subconsciously control our life and create self-fulfilling prophecies. Expectations are the master plans of our subconscious mind. It fuels your belief that you are a certain kind of person with a certain role. These expectations can either lead to your success or your failure. Expectations can either fill you with energy to achieve more or make you feel miserable and dissatisfied. Finding ways to change your expectations can be a powerful tool in mastering your mind and changing your life. Instead of expecting the worst-case scenario, what if you did the opposite? What if you expected success instead of failure?

The brain is also one of the most powerful parts of the human body. Boosting the power of the brain is essential for emotional health and in this case, to overcome negativity. If you want to feel better, feel happier, you need to *think about **what you're thinking about***. Your thoughts create your feelings which then create your behavior. When you're conscious of what you're thinking, you have the power to shift your feelings away from negativity. To boost your brain's power, you need to feed it with the most powerful force there is out there: *Positivity*.

Image source: <u>Buffer</u>

Boosting the power of your brain comes through repetition. The more you repeat positive reinforcement, the stronger and more resilient your brain then becomes. Your brain will always try to go with the easiest route that it knows, that's why you keep falling back on your old negative thought patterns. It's familiar, and you've been doing it for so long so to your brain, that feels like the easier path to take. Right now, you need to boost its resilience against such moments. Enhancing the brain's resilience and power against negativity comes from focusing on its counterpart. You want to get to a point in life where you automatically think about the best possible outcomes in any scenario you're thrown into.

The brain goes through an incredible 12,000 to 60,000 thoughts a day on average. The trouble is, some research speculates that at least 80% of these thoughts are biased toward the negative. Hence the need to train your brain and empower it for positivity.

- **Strengthen the Positive Memory -** It can be surprisingly helpful to equip your brain with a list of positive words that you've memorized. This exercise works by encouraging your brain to associate itself with the frequent use of positive dialogue so that when you think about retrieving an idea or word from memory, positive words start coming to mind. Another exercise in strengthening your brain's positive memory power is to frequently recall happy memories in your mind that make you feel good. When you think about these memories, describe them using the list of positive words you've come up with. This doubles as an exercise in training your brain's ability to focus on positivity.

- **Celebrating Your Successes** - Accomplishing any milestone in life is a cause for celebration. Whether big or small, it doesn't matter. What matters is you stop and take the time to appreciate your little victories. Get rid of the bad habit most of us are guilty of where we downplay the accomplishments we've achieved. If you put the effort in, then that's a *win*. Phrases like *"It's no big deal"* or *"Anyone could have done it"* are biased toward the negative. You're teaching your brain to minimize the positive emotions that it should be associating itself with.

- **Think of 3 Daily Positives** - Once you're ready to unwind for the day, think about three positive things that happened to you. That you feel happy and grateful for. Let your brain recall the specifics and immerse yourself in the memory again. It could be something as simple as not having to wait in line for your favorite cup of coffee, bumping into a friend you haven't seen in a while, a compliment you received today. Even on a rough day, there will be *something* good that happened, no matter how small the event may have been. This has the same effect as celebrating your successes, except this time, your daily habit is going to be celebrating the good things that happened to you.

How to Use Your Emotions and Mind to Grow

We're equipped with an innate drive for emotional growth. It exists, but because it remains unseen to the naked eye, we don't pay attention to this aspect of our development. We're naturally inclined to focus on our physical growth since that is the obvious one. We know what it means to be fully grown physically (from birth to adulthood), but what does it mean to be fully grown *emotionally*?

Not every emotion that we carry is fully acknowledged or understood. We carry around a lot of unprocessed feelings. Many worries may remain uninterpreted, manifesting as directionless anxiety. We fear what we don't fully understand and without fully processing these emotions, it can be difficult for the mind to grow. We become depressed when we don't know how to process our feelings of sadness in healthier ways. We struggle to sleep at night with the many unprocessed thoughts swimming around in our minds. We're afraid of our emotions because they could be at odds with the idea of who we want to be.

There's only one effective, surefire way to use our emotions to grow: *Emotional intelligence.* It is the only quality and skill that enables us to confront the many emotions we face with patience, insight, and understanding. It is a form of intelligence that does not currently enjoy the prestige that it should. We're so focused on intellectual intelligence that we forget there's a whole other side to ourselves that needs nurturing too. All the other success you enjoy will still leave you feeling empty if your emotional side does not enjoy the growth and development it should.

Self-awareness, self-regulation, social skills, empathy, and motivation. The five core skills of emotional intelligence and all five of which are needed to help you grow emotionally.

- **Self-awareness** brings the ability to accurately assess ourselves and gives us the advantage of being able to learn and improve every day.

- **Self-regulation** brings the advantage of being able to control our biological impulses so we're less filled with feelings of regret when we react in a way that we shouldn't. Self-regulation allows us to step back and understand *why* we're feeling a certain emotion, an essential skill needed for emotional growth.

- **Social skills** are the ability to build a rapport with others to move them in the desired direction. People with social skills are able to find common ground and build emotional bonds with others, and this positive rapport-building skill lead to satisfactory interpersonal relationships.

- **Empathy** is the ability to look beyond yourself and understand the emotions of others. With empathy, you're listening to what others have to say and putting yourself in their shoes. The ability to do that creates more fulfilling and meaningful relationships.

- **Motivation** involves a passion for anything that you undertake, and that passion will lead to a natural desire to raise your performance bar. You do better than you thought you would, and that cements confidence in your mind that you had it in you all along.

This is a skill that is going to change the way you see yourself, the people and the world around you. Your emotions will continue driving the bus if you let them. Once you understand your emotions, you're able to respond in more effective ways. When you no longer react impulsively and based on the spur of the moment without thinking it through, that's when you know you're on the right track toward emotional growth.

Conclusion

Thank you for making it through to the end of *Overcome Negativity*, let's hope it was informative and able to provide you with all of the tools you need to achieve your goals whatever they may be.

No matter how pessimistic you were before picking up this book, it's never too late to change the way you think. The only time it's going to become too late is when you give up and stop trying altogether. Every strategy you've covered in this book is designed to help pull your brain out of the negative zone it's stuck in, and pull it into a new zone of appreciation, gratitude, a change in your paradigm and becoming a more optimistic person overall.

In time, your brain will come to reflect a more positive outlook as your old habits slowly fade away. Research shows that it is possible to restructure your brain. Studies that have been carried out on those who participate in loving-kindness meditation for prolonged periods had thicker and denser neural activities in the area of the brain associated with happiness. In other words, it is possible to change the physical structure of your brain so that you're more inclined to feel happy.

This is wonderful news. It means with a little practice and using the strategies you've covered in the book, you, too, can start making serious changes in your brain. With a lot of practice, you can leave behind the negative personality you no longer want and create a new, better and more optimistic version of yourself.

Finally, if you found this book useful in any way, a review on Amazon is always appreciated!